Emotional Rescue

ALSO BY BEN GREENMAN

Fiction

Superbad

Superworse

A Circle Is a Balloon and Compass Both

Correspondences

Please Step Back

What He's Poised to Do

Celebrity Chekhov

The Slippage

Nonfiction

*Mo' Meta Blues: The World According to Questlove
(with Ahmir "Questlove" Thompson)*

*Brothas Be, Yo Like George, Ain't That Funkin' Kind of
Hard on You?: A Memoir (with George Clinton)*

I Am Brian Wilson (with Brian Wilson)

ESSAYS ON LOVE,
LOSS, AND LIFE — WITH
A SOUNDTRACK

Emotional Rescue

BEN GREENMAN

Little
a

Published by Little A, New York

www.apub.com

Amazon, the Amazon logo, and Little A are trademarks of Amazon.com, Inc., or its affiliates.

ISBN-13: 9781503934986 (hardcover)
ISBN-10: 1503934985 (hardcover)

ISBN-13: 9781503934979 (paperback)
ISBN-10: 1503934977 (paperback)

Cover design by Faceout Studio

Printed in the United States of America

To Gail, *who loves music as much as I do, and who I love as much as I love music.*

CONTENTS

INTRODUCTION
Why Songs Mean Everything
If You Let Them

SPARROW
Marvin Gaye — *Here, My Dear*
Tamla Motown: 1978

ONCE, IN AN OLD SHORT STORY I WROTE, A BIRD SANG WITHIN EARSHOT of a female character. The female character is waking up and thinking about what she wants to do with her day, and the singing bird gives her ideas. It is a small bird, and the song it sings is small, too, though the consequences of its singing are enormous. "The bird flew through a gap in the wire, minding its own business, singing—it was actually singing a happy little song about the spring—and she plugged it at two hundred yards." The way I see it, the bird and the woman are in a relationship, and this is the breakup scene. Bye-bye, birdie.

When I finished the story, I sent it off to the publisher for comments. I received one comment, which was that birds didn't sing when they flew. He had enough certainty to send me to the encyclopedia, where I quickly discovered that he was wrong. Many birds, including skylarks and pipits, sing while they're flying. In attempting to differentiate between the British chimney swallow and the American barn swallow, John James Audubon wrote in *Birds of America* that "both sing on the wing and when alighted, and the common tweet which they utter when flying off is precisely the same in both." They sing on the wing. That's a song in itself.

You may already know that this is a book about popular singers—which isn't to say pop singers—and the songs into which they poured their thoughts and feelings. I have listened to songs for almost as long as I have existed. I remember children's songs from when I was a child and then, soon after that, other songs. I haven't kept track of how many songs I have heard, but I do know that hundreds if not thousands have touched me at my core. I played them over and over again until

I learned all the words, until I knew when the drums came in, until I could name them when they came on the radio from just a few notes.

Songs started to mean everything to me. They contained so much wisdom about relationships, and I had none. For that matter, they contained relationships, and I had none. Whenever I heard songs—love songs from soul singers, bad-luck songs from pop singers, family songs from country singers—I took note of the way that the singer (had I been more sophisticated, I would have said the narrator, or the singer's character) interacted with friends or lovers. And then, as my own relationships began to develop, I looked back into the songs for points of contact. Whether with platonic friends or with romances, when I encountered moments I didn't quite understand—obstructions in the line—I turned to songs for help. The two things I thought the most about converged prophetically, if not profitably. The essays in this book, most of them very short, try to explore (and reward) the connection between pop songs and the labile emotional state of young adulthood. They follow a straightforward method. A certain number of songs are listed up top, and then enlisted to explore a topic. Maybe it's silence. Maybe it's honesty. Maybe it's doubt. The songs speak to the topic at hand, and also to each other.

These days, I am an old married man with two children. But I was not always old and married, and I wrote these pieces when I was changing from one kind of man into the other. It was years ago, and I wrote them in the moment, posting them to a website run by some friends called Moistworks.com (the name gave nearly everyone the willies). They were written with the music not only in mind, but in my mind—I listened to the songs as I wrote about the lyrics, and readers could listen to them with just a click or two. In trying to respect the fact that these pieces were born far in the past, a decade or more, I tried, when collecting and organizing them for this book, not to revise them too much, to keep both their freshness and some of their callowness.

The thoughts contained in them weren't forced to mature, which also means that they weren't allowed to ossify.

Many of these songs are love songs, because those are the songs that touch upon the rawest nerves. The wildest and wisest exploration of relationships I have ever heard is Marvin Gaye's *Here, My Dear*, which he released in 1978. He was on the brink of divorcing his first wife, Anna Gordy Gaye, who was the sister of Motown founder Berry Gordy. Anna was considerably older than Marvin. He was also well into a relationship with the woman who would become his second wife, Janis Hunter. (She was, like Anna, part of music royalty; her father was the brilliantly idiosyncratic jazz guitarist and singer Slim Gaillard.) As a result of various complicated alimony issues, the divorce was dragging. Gaye's lawyer convinced him to give up half of the royalties from his next album to Anna. The album that resulted from that odd arrangement was *Here, My Dear*, which not only funded the divorce, it dissected it.

Nearly every song on the album deals forthrightly with the questions that lurk inside every romantic relationship—and, in a different way, inside every relationship of any kind. There are songs about devotion, about loyalty, about trust, about distrust, about protection, about possessiveness, and about loneliness.

One of the minor songs from *Here, My Dear* is arguably its most beautiful: "Sparrow." In the song, Marvin explains that he "used to hear a sparrow singing," but that "one day as [he] went along [he] didn't hear his song." This silence doesn't sit well with him, and what starts as a polite request to the sparrow to resume singing becomes a down-on-my-knees-please entreaty. "Sing before you go," he sings. "Sing to me, Marvin Gaye, before you fly away." He's asking for a song.

> *Sing, little sparrow*
> *About the troubles you're in*
> *Places you've been*
> *You can sing, I know it*

Life is filled with confusion as well as places of comfort that give us safe haven from that confusion. Songs are one site of comfort, and the site that this collection maps. It's an investigation of ethical questions, friendship and relationship problems, anger, lust, guilt, and (sometimes) pleasure, but always with a soundtrack. "Sparrow" ends with a semi-attached bit of poetry, delivered by layered, lighter-than-air vocals: "I remember a bird."

All of these songs are birds, singing on the wing, remembered.

SUCCESS

Graham Parker — *The Mona Lisa's Sister*
RCA: 1988

ONE DAY THIS WEEK I WOKE UP TOO EARLY, STUBBED MY TOE, CUT myself shaving. Every clumsy bad-day cliché applied precisely. Other factors had conspired against me, too: I had received a note from a colleague who disapproved of something I had written, not because I had made a powerful argument that offended her sensibilities, but because she thought it just wasn't very good. Another older colleague whom I respect greatly suggested that the writing game has its limits, and that they are narrower than I might, even after doing it for fifteen years, suspect.

I read some authors that I love, which usually cheers me up, but it had the opposite effect, inspiring terror (and its crippled cousin, insecurity) that I might never get there myself. What resulted was displeasure with the wife, with the kids, with friends, with myself: a bad mood. I thought I'd get better soon enough. I didn't. Time passed, but not the mood. Nothing was working, so I turned to music. That's not surprising. But it was *how* I turned.

It is now well-known that technology has changed the way we listen to music. The change has been reported, analyzed, and accepted for some time now, as we have passed from pure push technology like radio (where you listen to what you're given) to technologies of increasing pull (LPs, where you have to lift a needle or flip a disc; CDs, where you can scan from track to track or, if you are crazy, program the playing order) to the pure-pull world of the i-streaming services and playlists. It's hard to imagine not being able to get exactly what you want. Do we want that? It's a question for another time.

One of the most obvious effects has been to eliminate the physical cost of carrying large amounts of music. In the old days, back when I couldn't wait for winter so that I could justify wearing a coat with pockets big enough to hold a Discman and a few CDs, I packed up with an eye toward variety. If I took a rock CD out with me, I tried to take a soul CD also, on the theory that moods are unpredictable, and I might get tired of one and need the other. If I took a CD with an aggressive vocalist, I tried to also take along something instrumental or soothing. If I took male singers, I took female singers. When I traded the Discman for the iPod, the first and most obvious effect was to atomize the album as the unit of music and give primacy to the song. Instead of listening to a James Brown album—never his strong suit—I could listen to eight or ten or twenty James Brown songs. This happened years ago. Remember? At the time it was a revolution. Now it's just a faint memory of when things used to turn.

The iPod and the MP3, and then streaming apps and streaming platforms, from Spotify to Sonos, have changed the way I respond to artists, some more than others. Some acts, like Randy Newman or ESG or Al Green, worked best in short bursts, a few songs at most, after which I had an itch to play something else. Technology encouraged extreme impatience—if a song wasn't aiding a good mood or counterweighting a bad one, it was simple to switch off—but that wasn't really the issue. Some artists were just better at the sprint. Maybe it was the richness of the aftertaste: It was difficult to hear Al Green sing "Jesus Is Waiting" (1973), the final song on *Call Me*, and not feel like everything else in his catalog was anticlimactic. Certain artists had always suggested other artists. Stevie Wonder made me want to hear Smokey Robinson. But with technology, the progression from one artist to another grew easier and easier. I loved visiting with these artists, but I found I couldn't stay.

Long before the PonoPlayer—in case you're not following the music press, that's the high-fidelity player that Neil Young plumped for over the course of 2015—lovers of music fought over whether songs optimized for MP3 download or for streaming (and thus lower quality) somehow encouraged skipping around. Were lower-quality songs somehow unable to grab listeners in the way that analog vinyl once did? What about AIFF? What about FLAC? I can't speak to any of that. I won't. I don't know the answers. I'm not even sure that I could tell the difference between vinyl and 320 kbps and hi-fi streaming. What I do know is that there are still certain artists who resist the process of compression and reward residency. When I listen to them, I want to listen to more of them, sometimes for days on end. *Pace* Yeats, the center holds.

Van Morrison has that effect. Sly Stone has that effect. The Ramones have that effect. Mary Margaret O'Hara, despite having a tiny body of work, has that effect. I want to draw a distinction, very important and possibly spurious, between the idea of an artist's quality and his or her ability to retain my attention for an extended period of time. I'm not arguing that Van Morrison is superior to Randy Newman or that I like him more, only that Van has a certain stickiness that keeps me in place while Randy has a certain re- or propulsive quality that sends me on to other artists. Whenever I come to an artist with stickiness or he or she comes to me, it has the feel of a weather event. It is a front that moves in from the west and hangs around for a while.

I raise the idea of weather events because I am currently in the middle of one. Last week, before the bad mood, everything seemed normal. I had loaded up my phone with music. Some days I go for streaming, but other days I resist and do what seems old-school at this point: I actually load files onto my phone. I let it run on random play. It skipped blithely from Panda Bear to Peaches to DMX to Kurt Vile to the Contours. Fine, iPhone. Pick what you want. I picked it first anyway. Then, during my bad mood day, my iPhone got stuck on Graham Parker. I'm not sure how. I was using a new app to play songs, and it had some shuffle-by-song setting I didn't know how to work properly, and so after the first Graham Parker song I got a second, then a third, then a fourth. I had about a hundred Graham Parker songs loaded up, more than six hours' worth, and so I went out for a walk, went to the gym, sat around the house with the iPhone steadily but randomly picking Graham Parker songs for me. Some songs weren't as good as I had remembered, particularly the more obscure album tracks from the seventies. Some of the vocal performances, particularly those from the nineties, were better than I had remembered. Some songs were too wordy. Some production choices were curious. But it was a relationship rather than a fling, and so his worldview began to both amplify and clarify mine, and I fell into the sound of his voice.

Somewhere along the way, I got "Success" (1988). It's from *The Mona Lisa's Sister*, an album that is often dismissed as uneven or underwritten when in fact it's neither. It's a strong set of songs, often superb, that are produced down close to the bone and share at least one unifying theme: The world will let you down if you let it.

This isn't a new theme in Parker's work, but it came at a time when he had left Atlantic Records under a cloud (after leaving Mercury Records under a cloud), and many of the lyrics are about an artist trying to find his place in a world populated by hostile (or, worse, indifferent) figures. The opening song, "Don't Let It Break You Down," and the single, "Get Started, Start a Fire," are both self-help texts, though particularly prickly and equivocal ones. The most striking song is "Success," which doesn't end the record but might as well, since it's followed by a bouncy minor number called "I Don't Know" and a beautifully sung if inessential cover of Sam Cooke's "Cupid."

"Success" opens with a strummed chord, some soothing harmonies, and a little lead guitar figure, all very nice and all utterly misleading given what Parker's singing about. He looks at the biggest version of the big picture, especially with regard to his own creative work, and he comes away stung.

> *The dreams and hopes of men are powered by addiction*
> *And who am I to say that this is an affliction*
> *When everybody gets suckered in and lives their lives like*
> *   fiction*

And what is this fiction that they're pursuing? It's not a spiritual system. It's not a romance—or rather, not necessarily. It's a fiction about the thing that people desire most, the core belief that seems to power contemporary society.

> *Writing their own stories of success*
>
> *They say they want you for your colorful evocation*
> *The way you turn a cliché into a sensation*
> *But all they ever wanted was that same vibration*
> *The one that shimmers round success*
>
> *Success success success success*
> *Success success success success*
> *All you ever need—success*
>
> *You can't be happy while someone else has a fistful*
> *They glow from TV screens: healthy, strong, and fiscal*

And everybody slaps their back while you're alone with a
    wristful
Jerking to the rhythm of success

When I first heard the record, I was eighteen and I was a little shocked by the last verse.

You can't be happy while someone else has a fistful
They glow from TV screens: healthy, strong, and fiscal
And everybody slaps their back while you're alone with a
    wristful
Jerking to the rhythm of success

The daring, even foolhardy rhymes (*fistful/fiscal?*) led directly to the final image, of Parker at home jerking off into the futility of his TV set, which carries a picture of somebody who's more famous. And then there's the way he pronounces the title: "suck-cess." It was brutal and remains so, although now the first and second verses, which are all about writing, cut just as deep. When I heard the song this week, in the middle of my bad mood, it reminded me that the bleakness of life takes many forms, and that none of those forms should be permitted to obscure the central mission, which is to record it honestly, powerfully, and continuously. That's how a song, or an artist, grabs you. That's, emotionally speaking, a fistful. The song meant more because of the Graham Parker songs before it and after it. It wasn't an argument against playlists, necessarily, but it was an argument for deeper engagement. That's, emotionally speaking, success.

HOTLINE BLING
Drake — Digital download / single
Cash Money: 2015

HELLO
Adele — 25
XL: 2015

BAD BLOOD
Taylor Swift — *1989*
Big Machine: 2014

WTF (WHERE THEY FROM)
Missy Elliott — Digital download / single
Goldmind/Atlantic: 2015

PRETTY PIMPIN
Kurt Vile — *b'lieve i'm goin down . . .*
Matador: 2015

FOR THE MOST PART, THE SONGS IN THIS BOOK ARE OLD, A FUNCTION of my inability to predict the future—when I wrote these essays, it was the past, and the songs of the present did not yet exist. It reminds me of a line in *Police Squad!*, the sitcom that evolved into the Naked Gun movies. Frank Drebin, the bumbling detective played by Leslie Nielsen, arrives at the home of a shooting victim. His widow answers the door in tears. "We're sorry to bother you at a time like this," Drebin says. "We would have come earlier, but your husband wasn't dead then."

If I had been able to look forward, many songs would have appealed to me. "Hotline Bling" (2015), for example, is about communication and disconnection, like much of this book, and consequently would have been hard to avoid. I might not have avoided it; there's a fascinating argument about language and communication in the misguided confidence of Drake's lyric "That can only mean one thing." It can?

That's comforting. And I could have definitely reckoned with Taylor Swift and Adele, at some level, if only to think about the fact that there are fewer and fewer inescapable mega-albums, fewer experiences that we all share. It used to be true that most of us were at least familiar with the top ten of any given week. That's not the case anymore. With fewer things in common, are the few things we have in common more important? And if that's so, what does it mean that the most successful albums are the ones that strike a tone of generic intimacy—autobiographically grounded albums written by young women who are fully aware of how to deploy their personal drama to the broadest effect. When Adele and Swift pull us into their worlds, we're powerless observers who are made to feel, via propaganda, that we're participants. "Who we used to be when we were younger and free"? "We got problems and I don't think we can solve 'em"?

Who's "we"? Missy Elliot's "WTF" (2015), a joyful and triumphant return to form even without its giddy video, has a guest rap from Pharrell Williams that mentions Hermes Trismegistus. That could have fit neatly into a longer piece about syncretic paganism.

But I didn't include any of those songs. I didn't write about them, apart from here. The relative scarcity of new pop material isn't only a function of the past's distance from the present. It's also part of the overall plan of the book. I have already discussed shifts in technology, and the way that streaming gives us access to everything while taking away the sense that we are engaged in something that's rewarding to access.

But the streaming world has another effect, which is that it radically democratizes time. As radio falters, as record stores vanish, as pull technology continues to push past push, it's as easy to find your way to a song from forty years ago as it is to find your way to a new song. Records that used to be difficult to locate are now on iTunes or Spotify right alongside the new Justin Bieber music. Well, "alongside" is a strange way to think about it. There's no physical shelf space. But they're all just a search away, whether Bieber or the Legendary Stardust Cowboy or Dan Hicks or Vic Mensa or Kamaiyah or Bobby Charles or Cool Uncle. Because of that, eclecticism is easier than ever—and because of that, the method of this book, which reflects my method of listening to music, is also easier than ever. Common threads can be identified and explored with great velocity. A song like Kurt Vile's "Pretty Pimpin" (2015)—in which the narrator stares unknowingly at himself in the mirror all week ("Then Saturday came around and I said, 'Who's this stupid clown blocking the bathroom sink?'") before experiencing equivocal self-knowledge ("But he was sporting all my clothes") and then a fleeting moment of ego ("I gotta say I'm pretty pimpin")—fits nicely into a tradition of other songs about identity that extends backward through Eminem's "The Real Slim Shady" (2000), Talking Heads' "Once in a Lifetime" (1981), Simon and Garfunkel's "I Am a Rock" (1966), and the Platters' "The Great Pretender" (1955). Collect them all. Listen in sequence. It'll only take a second. Hopefully, that's how the essays in this book will work. They will suggest surprising connections, coax axons toward new dendrites. At worst, they'll propose new sources of pleasure. We all employ (and are employed by) the same feelings, more or less. The older songs that accompany these essays are forever echoing in the songs of the present, and even the songs of the future. This will be the case until the species changes irretrievably. Until then, a man in a room with his hat in his hand, no matter what the month, no matter what the year, is thinking about the same kinds of things. Let him think.

Emotional
Rescue

COMMUNICATION/
MISCOMMUNICATION

THE LAST LETTER
Hank Snow
Released 1951
Available on: *The Thesaurus Transcriptions*
Bear Family: 1991

LETTERS DON'T COUNT
The Nazz — *Nazz Nazz*
Screen Gems Columbia: 1969

YOUR PICTURE SAYS REMEMBER, THO' YOUR LETTER SAYS FORGET
Frederic Rose
Edison Gold Moulded Record: 1908

I'VE GOTTA GET A MESSAGE TO YOU
The Bee Gees — *Idea*
ATCO: 1968

GOT TO GET A MESSAGE TO YOU
Swamp Dogg
Released 1970
Available on: *Total Destruction to Your Mind / Rat On*
Charly: 1991

I GOTTA GET A MESSAGE TO YOU
Tim Rose
Released 1970
Available on: *Tim Rose / Love: A Kind of Hate Story*
RPM: 2000

COMMUNICATION
Bobby Womack — *Communication*
United Artists: 1971

A BOOK ABOUT WRITING AND POP MUSIC SHOULD START WITH THE thing that's exactly midway between them: the letter. I don't mean the alphabet. I mean correspondence. I used to send lots of letters. In college, I had a girlfriend who went to another school, and sometimes each of us would mail three or four of them a day. The Internet did not exist back then, and we scooped food from stone bowls with our hands.

As soon as e-mail came along, though, things really took off, letter-wise. The problem wasn't sending messages. Not anymore. Rather, it was finding someone who was willing to get those messages and give the same back at a clip. The problem wasn't finding a way of corresponding. The problem was finding someone who corresponds to you.

It may seem that these issues are important only when it comes to love letters. It's not. It's true that "The Last Letter" (1951), by the great Canadian country singer Hank Snow, describes an eloquent, bitter, all-too-forthright communique that doesn't—as the last line tells us—hit its mark. And it's also true that the Nazz, and its front man, Todd Rundgren, better known for his long and willfully eclectic solo career (it continues to this day), turns a dopey pun into a beautiful piece of pop philosophy. And the composition that Frederic Rose wrote a million years ago, in 1908, elevates a B-list song with an A-list title. Back in college, we didn't send pictures. We just sent letters. These days, pictures are sent with an even more alarming regularity than letters.

Different writers. Different singers. Different eras. But underneath the surface, all these songs are about messages. They're not message songs, like "For What It's Worth" (1966) or "Fortunate Son" (1969) or "(We Gotta) Bust Out of the Ghetto" (1970) or "1 Million Bottlebags" (1991), but rather songs about the process of trying to reach out and communicate with another person, of sending up a flare and waiting for a response. And though there are probably a million places to start, there's really only one: "I've Gotta Get a Message to You" (1968).

I should begin by stipulating that this song has a story. The main character is condemned to die, and he's desperate to tell his wife that he's sorry and that he loves her. We know this because Robin Gibb has said that's what the song is about, and he cowrote it for the Bee Gees. This death-row-what-a-brother-Gibb-know plotline, though, is among the worst things about the song. For starters, it results in some laughably bad lyrics, which sometimes happens with the Gibbs.

It's only her love that keeps me wearing this dirt.

Dirt aside, I like to think of it as something more epistolary and epistemological, a song about the urgency and imprecision of communication. Partly it's because there is something interesting about the syntax. The man in the song is not saying, "I've got to get a message to her." He's saying "to you." This seems to be an internal monologue; he's talking to that part of her that is alive inside of him. The alternative is paradoxical. If his wife hears the song, or any part of it, then she has in fact received a message from him. In that case, he might as well say what he wants to say instead of just saying that he has a message. It's like sending a telegram that says, "I am trying to send you a telegram." And given his precarious state, even if she hears the song, she is certainly hearing it after his execution. There's an issue here not only of the man's death but also of his death as an author. I'm not saying that my logic is flawless, only that the song's logic is flawed.

So why is it so hard to get a message to, or through to, someone else? Why is it so difficult to be heard, let alone understood? One of the problems is that most forms of expression are insufficient. There's the famous Gustave Flaubert passage in which he decries the impotence of language ("Language is a cracked kettle on which we beat out tunes for bears to dance to, while all the time we long to move the stars to pity"). I'm not sure that it's the bears that are dancing. I'd argue that just as often, it's the messenger—whoever is beating on the cracked kettle. People are afraid to say the things they mean to say, and so they hem, and they haw, and they hint around the edges. That's how more language is born, isn't it? I'm not suggesting that all writing is evasion, but most works could be shorter if they were more direct. That kind of directness might normally result from a sudden bravery, or from painful impatience, or from another kind of urgency—like, say, imminent execution, though we've already seen how circuitous a condemned man can be.

If I always had to say just what I meant, things would be . . . well, different. There would be a little more lust, a little more anger, and fewer jokes. Much of what I'd say would involve my asking people to say things back to me: anything, really, just a conversation (with words, gestures, touch, whatever) so that I know I'm not dead. If I rewrote the Bee Gees' lyrics, they'd go like this:

> *I've just gotta get a message to you*
> *Which is that you've gotta get a message to me*

No worse.

Of the three versions here, my tastes lean toward the Swamp Dogg cover, which is sung with a kind of abject ecstasy, and away from the original—chamber pop, no matter how tremulous, doesn't strike me as a particularly lonely genre. Tim Rose, on the other hand, does. Rose, of course, was one of those semi-obscure Greenwich Village folk-rockers— the third Tim, behind Buckley and Hardin—and King of the Almosts. He *almost* had a hit with his slow arrangement of "Hey Joe" (1966), which inspired the monster hit by Jimi Hendrix (1966). He *almost* recorded the headlong version of "With a Little Help from My Friends" that went to Joe Cocker instead (1969). He *almost* replaced Brian Jones in the Rolling Stones. His life of ups and downs, marked by bouts of alcoholism, ended during a late-career comeback in 2002.

Tim Rose would recognize that this section is almost over. He might also recommend ending on a song that handles the issue of evasion by illustrating the benefits of directness. And the messenger for that message is Bobby Womack, who never had trouble making himself known. Womack, a great soul singer, was also a talented monologist who spoke extended intros before suddenly (and surprisingly) launching into song. Here, he mostly just launches.

FRIENDSHIP/SELF-INTEREST

GREAT EXPECTATIONS

Miles Davis
Released 1969
Available on: *The Complete Bitches Brew Sessions*
Columbia Legacy: 1998

YOUR ENEMY CANNOT HARM YOU (BUT WATCH YOUR CLOSE FRIEND)

Rev. Edward W. Clayborn
Released 1927
Available on: *Goodbye, Babylon*
Dust-to-Digital: 2003

(SHE'S SO) SELFISH

The Knack — *Get the Knack*
Capitol: 1979

SHE'S MY BEST FRIEND

Lou Reed — *Coney Island Baby*
RCA Victor: 1976

MY FRIENDS HAVE

Marianne Faithfull — *Before the Poison*
Anti-: 2005

OLD FRIENDS

Willie Nelson (with Roger Miller and Ray Price)
Released 1982
Available on: *One Hell of a Ride*
Columbia Legacy: 2008

LONG AGO, MY LIFE BOTHERED ME. IT WASN'T GOING WELL, IN VARIOUS ways. I grew irritated and then depressed. There was only one solution, which was to go on a walk with my iPod. That's how we listened to music back then, disconnected from the giant sentient squid we today call the Internet. You can read about iPods in the history books. Books were like packs of paper stapled together.

My iPod was empty except for one playlist of especially long songs. They were intended to calm me down. One of them was Miles Davis's "Great Expectations," which he recorded during the *Bitches Brew* sessions and later released on *Big Fun*. The desired effect was not what I got. I found myself thinking about the title rather than the music— occupational hazard—and how many of life's disappointments result from unmanaged expectations. I went home and became progressively more agitated. Who can say why? I couldn't say why.

I called a friend to complain. I picked the friend of mine who disappointed me the least. We had dated briefly. "Very briefly," she said whenever I said it, and that made me laugh. I could usually count on her to make me laugh or remind me that the world has things in it that were worthy of laughter. That day was different. She answered her phone curtly. "What's up?" she said. I said that I was bothered by something but couldn't quite figure it out. She said she'd have to call back. She was working on a writing project and waiting on a call from an insect expert.

"An expert on insects or an expert who is an insect?" I said.

"I have to go," she said.

While I was waiting for her to get back to me, I became annoyed again, not at the world but at myself. I had allowed myself to have high expectations of her, and she hadn't lived up to them. Then I got annoyed at her. Were my expectations so high? I was feeling bothered, and I wanted a sympathetic ear, not an ear connected to a body that was preoccupied with an insect expert. Mostly, I resented the fact that by ending the conversation without really talking to me, she had created an imbalance that, for a few minutes, seemed grave. I didn't usually call her. She usually called me. On days when she wasn't very busy, she called me all the time. Reasons varied. Maybe one day she was in a fight with her brother. Maybe another day she was excited to tell the story of a bad date. Maybe a bird had just flown by her window and given her a dirty look. I didn't mind listening. I liked it. But when the shoe was on the other hand, when I needed her to talk to me, even for a moment, there was nothing there for me.

What do you do when you're feeling this way? In my youth, I had been known to kick a chair or say cruel things to people nearby. In my wisdom, I listened to music instead. I started with Robert Johnson's "When You Got a Good Friend," which seems to be a song about treating those close to you well until you get to the third verse.

> *Mmm, baby, I may be right or wrong*
> *Baby, it's your opinion, I may be right or wrong*
> *Watch your close friend, baby, then your enemies can't do*
>   *you no harm*

Johnson was taking up a theme articulated in other records of the twenties and thirties, most notably the preaching blues "Your Enemy Cannot Harm You (But Watch Your Close Friend)" by Edward W. Clayborn, which seems mostly like a big I-told-you-so to Jesus but also states explicitly that close friends have access to parts of you that others do not, and that they are able to use that access for either good or for evil.

> *People, I want to tell you*
> *Just how your friend will do*
> *They will wait to get your secret*
> *And dig a pit for you*

Those lines started me thinking. What finished me thinking was the Knack's "(She's So) Selfish," which sketches out a related (if far more carnal) problem.

> *Day after day after day after night after night after night*
> *You've been giving her what she wants*
> *Is she giving you what you need*
> *No way*

The song is four and a half minutes long, and the impulse to think of my friend in its light had dulled by the third minute, mainly because I remembered that everyone is selfish, and everyone knows that everyone else is, too. If I like listening to my friend's problems and want to hear more of them as a result, doesn't that make me just as selfish as she is, but with a different agenda?

I became more reasonable. I couldn't help it. I took a walk and listened to Lou Reed's "She's My Best Friend," especially that part when he sings "she understands me when I'm feelin' down" (or, if you'd prefer the Velvet Underground's version, "fallin' down"). I calmed down into circumspection, and that led to rhetorical questions. Did I have the right to feel annoyed I wasn't a higher priority that day for my friend? Of course. Did I have the right to say anything about it? No. Was I aware that any real friendship is the average of those days when you're not the other person's priority and the days when the other person isn't your priority? Not really—I wasn't that smart. But I found a song that summed it up nicely: "My Friends Have," which P. J. Harvey wrote and Marianne Faithfull sang. Like many Faithfull songs, it expressed a fairly straightforward sentiment but turns it on its head with her blasted vocals.

> *My friends have many features*
> *Many reasons, I can believe them*

My friends have many things that
I am needing, to keep me singing

Eventually my friend called back. We had a nice conversation. I accused her of being a jerk for not coming through but admitted that I was a jerk for expecting too much. That was years ago. We've had the same conversation or a variation on it several times. Over the years, I have come to the galling realization that as I have aged, I need people more. And not people in the abstract: certain people. Friends used to be more fungible: If one went missing, I'd pick up the thread with another one. But then you settle into yourself, and you meet your wife, and you have children, and time sifts whether you want it to or not, and most friends recede. Those few who remain become permanently, irreversibly important. You can act casual. You should. Admitting that other people are important to your survival can feel a little embarrassing, even more so if it's true. I can't predict the future at all, so I can't predict the future of the friendship. But I'm entitled to my hope, no matter how prognostically nostalgic and mawkish. And in the same spirit, I'm entitled to "Old Friends"—not the Simon and Garfunkel hit, but a Roger Miller song on which he's joined by Willie Nelson and Ray Price.

Old friends
Pitching pennies in the park
Playing croquet till it's dark

It ends with a prayer, which is also a request. It seems simple. It is simple. But is it simple to grant?

Lord, when all my work is done
Bless my life, grant me one
Old friend

EFFORT/EASE

KEEP A KNOCKIN'
Little Richard
Released 1957
Available on: *Little Richard: The Georgia Peach*
Specialty: 1991

KEEP A KNOCKIN' BUT YOU CAN'T COME IN
Louis Jordan and His Tympani Five
Released 1939
Available on: *Louis Jordan and His Tympani Five*
JSP: 2001

LET THEM KNOCK
Sharon Jones and the Dap-Kings — *100 Days, 100 Nights*
Daptone: 2007

KEEP A KNOCKIN'
The Sonics
Released 1964
Available on: *Here Are the Sonics!!!*
Norton: 1998

KEEP A'KNOCKIN'
Mott the Hoople — *Wildlife*
Atlantic: 1971

KEEP A KNOCKIN' (take 1)
Little Richard
Recorded 1957
Available on: *The Specialty Sessions*
Specialty: 1990

KEEP A KNOCKIN' (take 2)
Little Richard
Recorded 1957
Available on: *The Specialty Sessions*
Specialty: 1990

KEEP A KNOCKIN' (take 3)
Little Richard
Recorded 1957
Available on: *The Specialty Sessions*
Specialty: 1990

KEEP A KNOCKIN' (take 4)
Little Richard
Recorded 1957
Available on: *The Specialty Sessions*
Specialty: 1990

AT HALF PAST TWO IN THE AFTERNOON ON A SUMMER DAY EARLIER IN this century, a repairman came to fix the buzzer at my apartment. I believe his name was Bill. Bill looked at the buzzer box, then at the door. He untwisted some wires and retwisted some others. It still didn't work. "Why don't people just knock?" he said. It sounded almost like he didn't want the work. When he left, though, his question still hung there, wires out.

In songs, people do knock. Knocking has been part of the blues, R&B, soul, and rock and roll as long as there's been blues, R&B, soul, and rock and roll. There's Mississippi John Hurt's "Keep on Knocking." There's Lazy Lester's "I Hear You Knockin'" (1959). There's the Rolling Stones' "Can't You Hear Me Knocking." There's "I Hear You Knocking" and "Knock on Wood" and "Knockin' on Heaven's Door." But mainly, truly, there's Little Richard's "Keep a Knockin'." Originally recorded in September 1957, the song opens with one of the most famous bits of drumming in rock and roll. (In fact, it became "Rock and Roll" when Led Zeppelin stole it wholesale.) About thirty seconds into the song, Little Richard, who has evidently been trapped in a soundproof glass box until then, bursts into the song with superhuman and possibly inhuman intensity. There are many songs that people point to as the beginning of rock and roll. Some people say Jackie Brenston's "Rocket 88" (1951). Some people say Bill Haley's "Rock Around the Clock" (1955). But sit those people in front of "Keep a Knockin'" and watch it blow back their hair. It may not have gotten there first, but it got there quicker and meaner.

> *Keep a knockin' but you can't come in*
> *Come back tomorrow night and try it again*

"Keep a Knockin'" wasn't original, of course. It was an old Louis Jordan number from 1939 that goes back even further, to Lil Johnson's "Keep on Knocking" in 1935. At that time, the (double) meaning was clear: It's a woman singing and a man knocking, and what he's knocking on is her front door (you know—the kind of door you can slide a key into and out of until that key ejaculates), and she's not letting him in no matter how much he knocks, so he might as well not even bother. This has been taken up recently, with Sharon Jones and the Dap-Kings' excellent "Let Them Knock" (2007).

> *Let them knock upon my door until their hands are black-*
> > *and-blue*
> *I'm not answering for no one until my man and I are*
> > *through*

When the gender switches, and it's a man singing, the knocking is a little stranger. Is it a woman knocking? How persistent is she? And why does the man have to bar the door, anyway? And when it's Little Richard singing, the strangeness turns into something tremendous— something threatening and seductive and terrified and terrifying, all at the same time. The same theme recurs in other Little Richard songs, like "Heeby-Jeebies" from the previous year, where he says, somewhat sadistically, that he's going to "ring your door till I break your bell." These songs rarely raise the issue of Little Richard's sexual orientation, even obliquely, but they frequently raise the issue of his sexual aggressiveness. If Louis Jordan swings, Little Richard swings a hammer.

"Keep a Knockin'" is a nearly perfect hit all on its own, but it's even more perfect when you relive that nuclear two and a half minutes with the various takes on the *Specialty Sessions* box set. Imagine being in the studio, hearing the explosive vocals of the first take, and then calling for a second take. And then a third. And then a fourth. Hearing them in series is like taking a car up to a hundred, smashing it into a wall, and then heading right back to the drag strip. It just doesn't seem possible.

Plenty of people have covered "Keep a Knockin'": Buddy Holly, Jerry Lee Lewis, Doug Sahm, the Everly Brothers, Suzi Quatro. It may be easier to list the bands that haven't covered it, and then to try to make sense of the oversight. Of all of the covers, there are two that deserve honorable mention. First, there's the version by the ultimate garage band, the Sonics (1964), whose lead vocalist, Gerry Roslie, does such a convincing job replicating Little Richard's carnal fury that he transcends imitation or parody and creates one of the great monuments of white R&B. And then there's the marathon ten-minute live version by Mott the Hoople (1971), which incorporates pieces of "I Got a Woman," "Whole Lotta Shakin' Going On," and "What'd I Say," and serves as a capstone to the otherwise subdued album *Wildlife*.

I remember once, years ago, I was starting to date a woman. This was in Miami, and we were in her apartment, watching some old movie on TV. I was dozing off, or at least pretending to, and when I seemed plausibly half-asleep, I reached over and flopped a hand onto her thigh. Where the hands of a sleeping man will go, who can know? She picked my hand up, put it back in my lap, and laughed. "Come back tomorrow night and try it again," she said. Love bloomed instantly.

LIKE/LOVE

VERSES FROM THE ABSTRACT
A Tribe Called Quest — *The Low-End Theory*
Jive: 1991

SUMMER ROMANCE
The Rolling Stones — *Emotional Rescue*
Rolling Stones: 1980

LOVE GETS YOU TWISTED
Graham Parker — *Squeezing Out Sparks*
Arista: 1979

I DON'T LOVE YOU BUT I THINK I LIKE YOU
Gilbert O'Sullivan
Released 1975
Available on: *Greatest Hits*
Rhino: 1991

SOMEONE I CARE ABOUT
The Modern Lovers — *The Modern Lovers*
Home of the Hits: 1976

I CAN'T KEEP FROM CRYIN' SOMETIMES
Davy Graham
Released 1964
Available on: *Folk, Blues, and Beyond . . .*
Fledg'ling: 2005

SOME PEOPLE LIKE TO HEAR ABOUT HAPPINESS. THEY ARE NOURISHED by stories about joy and satisfaction. Others, not so much. Back in Chicago, when I was a graduate student, I had a friend who loved hearing stories about relationships gone bad. She was the one I went to when it happened to me, which was more often than I would have liked. I nicknamed her "Ann Slanders," because when she gave advice, it usually came with a stick of dynamite taped to it. She liked telling me that as long as I kept being stupid, I was never going to be smart.

Usually, she directed her venom outward. But one night, after a few beers, she blew up at herself. "I'm no good at this," she said. What she meant was something different. She was good at having friends but a bust at everything else, and she felt an encroaching despair about it. For months, she said, she had been following a pattern whose returns had diminished to nearly nothing. "I can't keep from crying sometimes," she said.

"Let me get another beer and I'll be right back," I said. I got a pint. It seemed like it might take a while.

She explained the pattern when I returned. She hadn't had many real boyfriends. "It's not hard to see why," she said. "People are idiots. I dare you to disagree."

"Go on," I said.

"So in lieu of boyfriends, there are boys. Do you know what I mean?"

"You mean for sex?"

"Not just," she said. "Romance, too. But yes—that thing that makes my brain sing." A Tribe Called Quest was on the jukebox, and she told me about her favorite line from "Verses from the Abstract" (1991).

> *Girls love the jim 'cause it causes crazy friction*
> *When it goes up in and fluctuates the diction*

""Cause it causes'?" I said.

"Anyway," she said, "let's stay on point. Bringing guys home now and then is fun enough, but it leaves something to be desired."

"It happens to everyone," I said. "Nothing works until the thing that works. And who's to say that they're not first tier?" I tried to make my tone generous, though the fact was that I thought her picks were fourth tier at best. The most recent guy, whom she had met in line at a bagel store, had come with her to a party and told everyone who would listen that he was a "sonic manager." The big project he was dreaming of was about "how America is really all sounds—you could close your eyes and listen better and know exactly where you were."

"I'm to say," she said. "But that's not the worst part. The worst part is that I can't limit my expectations. I tell everyone, including myself, that I only want these guys as placeholders, but then I dream about all of them becoming something more. The second I get even slightly comfortable with them, I'm mad that I'm with someone who makes me feel comfortable. There aren't fireworks."

"Maybe you should start with something that's something."

"I should," she said. "But not how you're saying it." She had spotted a hue in my tone that she didn't like. "It's not like you're in some wonderful relationship." That wasn't true. I was, or thought I was. Time would prove me wrong. But time hadn't happened yet.

We sat in silence. Now the Rolling Stones were on the jukebox: "Undercover of the Night." I quoted another Stones song back to her, "Summer Romance" from *Emotional Rescue*. It wasn't much of a song, but she had told me she was in despair, and I was trying to buoy her mood.

Just a few days and you'll be back in your school
I'll be sitting around by the swimming pool

But it doesn't end well.

It's over now, it's a summer romance and it's through

"Yeah, well, if it's romantic advice you're looking for, you should definitely listen to Mick Jagger," she said.

"Or to you."

"That's not nice."

"No," I said. "It's not." This brought on a sort of deadlock. We sat there silently for a little while longer.

"I just think that I deserve love," she said.

"Of course you do," I said. "Everyone does." But I was just talking. I didn't know if everyone did. And what was love anyway? My Bloody Valentine was on the jukebox at that point. It was "Only Shallow" (1991), a song I didn't know very well, but the band's name put me in mind of Graham Parker's "Love Gets You Twisted" (1979).

> *Love gets you twisted, love gets you twisted all the way*
> *The hearts are enlisted, the hearts are enlisted to break*
> *each day*

Is that what she wanted? Who wanted to be twisted?

"What?" she said. I hadn't realized I was speaking out loud. Somewhere along the way I had downed another pint, and there was another full glass on the table in front of me. Had I gone back to the bar? I was drunk, or getting there, and Ann was starting to look better and better. "What?" she said. Had I said that out loud, too? "What are you thinking?" she said. I wasn't. I took another sip of beer. I wasn't even twenty-five yet. I was no philosopher. Worse, I was not being a good friend. She had asked me for a solution to her problem: How could she break the cycle of inadequate men? The only answer I could come up with was a bad one, in the sense that it was not about her but about me. Gilbert O'Sullivan's "I Don't Love You But I Think I Like You" (1975) wasn't on the jukebox. I don't even think it was in the jukebox. But it had some lines that I was thinking about.

> *If there's a question you'd like to make*
> *It really depends on how much it weighs*

That evening in the bar ended blearily. I didn't have any idea how she could find her way to men who meant more to her. We stood and made to leave. "This song is great," she said, gesturing to the jukebox.

"It is," I said. A few minutes later, I'd forget what the song even was. A few hours later, we'd be standing in front of her house, and I'd have my hand in her hair. A few weeks later, we'd sleep together. A few months later, after countless awkward attempts to broach the subject of what we both agreed was a terrible mistake, we'd see less and less of each other, until the friendship flickered and died.

Years later I heard that Ann Slanders got married. No one else knew her by that nickname. It was an inside joke, purely so. A mutual friend who attended the wedding told me that at the reception, she asked how I was doing.

"What did you say?" I said.

"I said fine," he said, sounding surprised.

"What's the husband like?"

"Nice guy," he said. "They were friends first."

"She always said that she wanted someone she felt comfortable with," I said. This was a lie, of course—she had said the opposite—but I felt okay about correcting for wisdom. I went back home and listened to the Modern Lovers' "Someone I Care About" (1976), in which Jonathan Richman longs for meaning in addition to sex. It was a song I associated with my short romance with her, but what was more interesting was what I had missed in the process. In the song, Richman doesn't devalue the friends who can't be his lovers so much as the lovers who can't be his friends.

> Well, I don't want a triumph in the car
> I don't want to make a rich girl crawl
> What I want is a girl that I care about
> Or I want no one at all

Time has passed and passed again, and it's hard to call anything from so long ago a regret, but there's always something a little sad when a song fades out. I would have liked to have been at her wedding, one way or another, and for her to have been at mine. I should have closed my eyes and listened better and known exactly where I was.

TRUST/DISTRUST

TRUST
The Pretty Things — *S.F. Sorrow*
Columbia: 1968

IT DON'T COME EASY
George Harrison
Demo recorded 1970

YOU'RE UP TO YOUR SAME OLD TRICKS AGAIN
Bettye Swann
Released 1969
Available on: *Bettye Swann*
Astralwerks: 2004

ILL PLACED TRUST
Sloan — *Never Hear the End of It*
Sony BMG: 2006

TRUST IN ME
The Fall — *Fall Heads Roll*
Narnack: 2005

FRIENDS
The Beach Boys — *Friends*
Capitol: 1968

DURING THE RECENT HOLIDAY SEASON I RECONNECTED WITH SOME people I hadn't talked to in a while. One of those people lives far away. Our friendship has spanned two decades, four cities, and countless jobs and relationships. "Did you get the present I sent you?" I said.

"You sent me a present?"

"I'm joking," I said. We had made that joke before, many times, to one another.

"I should know better than to trust you," she said.

Her tone was light, but the message thudded between us. All of a sudden, I was exhausted. "I'm sorry," I said, though I was lamenting more than apologizing. Why has she not always trusted me? Well, look. It's none of your business. I think we can all agree on that. I'll only say that there have been periods where we did not treat each other well. My intentions were good, but as my imaginary rural grandmother likes to say, "Good intentions are like an empty milking bucket." Was the breach irreparable? Would she ever trust me again? Was she even serious? That night, I walked around Brooklyn for a while, lamenting further, armed with songs.

"It Don't Come Easy" (1970) is best known, of course, in the version sung by Ringo Starr. Ringo, post-Beatles, got by with a little help from his friend George Harrison, who made a demo and sent it to Ringo in the mail. George's demo is more winsome and more weary. It's a love song, in a sense, but there's one lyric that bears upon the discussion I was having with my friend.

> *I don't ask for much*
> *I only want your trust*

How naïve and cynical at the same time. How George. I don't really appreciate that he raises the issue without solving it, but maybe that's his way of getting me to think for myself.

How do you get someone to trust you? Well, here's part of an answer: If you say you want to meet for lunch, don't show up an hour late, remark that you're not hungry, and keep looking at your watch. That's not going to create the kind of foundation you need, as Bettye Swann points out. (Oddly, "You're Up to Your Same Old Tricks Again" was originally written and recorded by John D. Loudermilk two years earlier. In his version, the untrustworthy party is a woman.) And don't embark upon an aggressive campaign of lying and cheating as outlined in the Sloan song (though Sloan also suggests that maybe the person who is incapable of trust necessarily establishes a climate where trust is impossible—you know, because of the creeping paranoia).

These trust songs are, for the most part, love songs. The friend I was fighting with wasn't a lover. So why was trust so difficult to repair? Shouldn't friendship be easier than love? I went home, and my iPod and I looked around for pop songs about trust in platonic friendships. They weren't as easy to find. Maybe the stakes are judged too low. Maybe when we hear pop songs playing, we want to imagine them ending in a kiss, or in bed. I eventually found the Fall's "Trust in Me," which may or may not have a romantic component but doesn't handle it straightforwardly, at any rate.

> *If you need an X-ray*
> *I will come to your house and do it for free*

What a generous offer. You never know when you'll need an X-ray. Actually, when you think about it for a while, the line starts to seem less platonic. Luckily, there was Brian Wilson—or, more specifically, the Brian Wilson of "Friends," vulnerable, troubled, and brilliant.

> *We've been friends now for so many years*
> *We've been together through the good times and the*
> *tears . . .*
> *Dim dipple ee dim dipple ay dim dipple oo dim dee aye oh*

Leaving aside the meaning of the last line, there's a comfortable complacency to the rest of the sentiment. The role of trust in this friendship isn't even raised. It's just assumed. Maybe it's part of "the tears." But maybe not. Maybe there's always been trust between Brian Wilson and his friend. When I listened to the song again, I started to think that maybe there's something to be said for gentle presumption. My faraway friend and I could have benefited from it repeatedly over the years. When I have gotten into the chicanes of distrust with her, I have tried to maneuver my way out aggressively. I have yelled, "Hey, you should trust me!" This turns out to be stupid. If you try to compel someone else to trust you, you may well be indulging in a kind of bullying that erodes the very trust you are trying to build. I am sure that she has explained this to me, but sometimes it's hard to understand things unless they're put plainly. "Dim dipple ee dim dipple ay dim dipple oo dim dee aye oh."

PAIN/PLEASURE

SAILOR'S GRAVE ON THE PRAIRIE
Tinsley Ellis — *Cool on It*
Landslide: 1986

THE SAILOR'S GRAVE ON THE PRAIRIE
Leo Kottke — *6- and 12-String Guitar*
Takoma: 1969

DARK IS THE NIGHT
Ry Cooder — *Ry Cooder*
Reprise: 1970

DARK WAS THE NIGHT—COLD WAS THE GROUND
Blind Willie Johnson
Released 1927
Available on: *The Complete Blind Willie Johnson*
Columbia Legacy: 1993

DIMMING OF THE DAY / DARGAI
Richard and Linda Thompson — *Pour Down Like Silver*
Island: 1975

DARGAI
J. Scott Skinner
Recorded 1922
Streaming Audio Excerpt

LATE LAST WEEK I GOT A BIG HEADACHE. I NEVER HAVE HEADACHES, SO it was annoying. More annoying was the fact that it didn't go away after aspirin, after an hour, after the morning. I started worrying about worst-case scenarios: meningitis, aneurysm, tumor. Like I said, I never get headaches. I was fighting with my wife, but that didn't seem like the cause of it. The weather was terrible. Was I that suggestible? I didn't know: maybe. What I did know was that the headache took away my ability to listen to music. Suddenly, everything—drums, horns, even

Bobby Womack's voice—was too much. Rather than give up, I used my affliction as a filter, and went in search of the most soothing music in my collection.

Back in the eighties, when I used to buy music for art, I picked up an album because its record jacket featured a picture of a snake charmer. It turned out to be a pretty good blues record by an Atlantan named Tinsley Ellis. I listened to it a few times, after which I would have set it aside had it not been for the fifth track, which was a beautiful instrumental. As it turned out, it was a cover of a song from Leo Kottke's debut album. I went and found that version, too, and over time I leaned toward it. It wheezed and rattled more than the Ellis, like the sonic equivalent of a vintage automobile, and as a result was easier to love, especially in the era of the Thompson Twins and Duran Duran. I tried to treat my headache with both versions of the song. They took the edge off but left a dull pain.

Dull pain crystallized into a sharp memory. When I was fourteen, I house-sat for friends of the family, which basically meant that my parents let me stay in a house a few blocks away by myself for a weekend. This was in Miami. What did a young house-sitting man do in Miami back then, in the eighties? He ordered pizza and watched OnTV, which was a precursor to HBO. He also made cassette copies of records, including Ry Cooder's debut, which consisted mostly of covers of songs by old bluesmen like Blind Alfred Reed and Sleepy John Estes. The last song on the record arrested me. It was an instrumental, a strange one, much more primal than the rest. I made up my mind to get the original. In those days, before the Internet, it took weeks—suburban record stores didn't have extensive blues sections.

When I finally heard Blind Willie Johnson's version, I was amazed. It made Ry Cooder's cover sound like it was performed by Josie and the Pussycats, and I mean no disrespect to Ry Cooder (or, for that matter, Josie and the Pussycats). It was just so much deeper, so much more mysterious, so much more terrifying, so much . . . more. When

I listened to "Dark Was the Night—Cold Was the Ground" (1927), I knew that it wouldn't take my headache away, but I thought it might remind me of the fleeting nature of the entire physical realm. Nearly everyone who has written about the song uses the word *spiritual*, and that's an understatement. It's truly awe-inspiring. It is capable of inspiring actual and lasting transcendence. It's also somewhat well-known at this point, but so is the Bible.

In the end, the only salve was Richard Thompson's "Dargai" (1975). Thompson plays it beautifully, but he didn't write it. That honor goes to James Skinner, who was born in Aberdeenshire, Scotland, in 1843. In his youth, Skinner played the cello and fiddle at dances, and in his early teens he became a champion Highland dancer under the instruction of William Scott (he added Scott's name to his own in tribute). Starting around 1860, Skinner also began to compose, eventually writing more than six hundred pieces of music. "Dargai," which was written in 1900 to commemorate the storming of Dargai Heights by the Gordon Highlanders during the second Afghan War, kicked around for most of the twentieth century, turning up here and there on classical or Celtic recordings. Then, in 1975, Richard Thompson gave it a definitive reading when he linked it to the final song on his album *Pour Down Like Silver*. The song, "Dimming of the Day," is already almost unspeakably sad. In it, his wife Linda considers a lover that she cannot have.

> *I'm living for the night we steal away*
> *I need you at the dimming of the day*

As "Dimming of the Day" dims, it sets into the gentle night of "Dargai," which lasts for three and a half minutes that I wish were thirty. It's an instrumental, stately and meditative without being static, and while some people may hear the same thing and call it gloomy, some people are wrong. "Dargai" cured my headache entirely.

I liked to play "Dargai" whenever I could, at least for a while. During that period, a friend called me to lament that her life was a mess. Her boyfriend had called from another city to tell her that he was in love with someone else and wouldn't be seeing her anymore. She was sobbing loudly. She said she wished it had never happened. I agreed, especially after twenty more minutes of her sobbing. She asked me a number of questions I could not possibly have answered. Had she done something wrong? Why was he oddly indifferent to sex? Did I think they might have made it, after all, and had children? I didn't know what to say. I didn't say much. She hung up eventually, still crying. I should have recommended "Dargai."

DISTANCE/NEARNESS

STRANDED IN THE JUNGLE
The Cadets
Released 1956
Available on: *The Doo Wop Box III: 101 More Vocal Group Gems*
Rhino: 2000

STRANDED IN THE JUNGLE
The New York Dolls — *Too Much Too Soon*
Mercury: 1974

STRANDED IN THE JUNGLE (live)
The New York Dolls — *From Paris with Love (L.U.V.)*
Sympathy for the Record Industry: 2002

THE PROCESS OF COMMUNICATION IS ALMOST ALWAYS COMPLICATED BY circumstance, and motive, and chance. One of the most obvious truths you'll hear is that it's easier to communicate with someone when you're close to them. This is true, though no one really knows what the word *close* means in this context. I had a girlfriend once when I was very young, and she believed that our conversations were perfect. I wanted to believe it, too. But the first time we were separated, it became clear that things were far from perfect. We didn't connect on the telephone. She felt like she wasn't getting what she wanted from me. She couldn't articulate her complaint exactly, but she articulated it well enough. She seemed to feel I was removed, and more removed than the physical distance allowed. When she got back from her trip, she raised the issue again. Specifically, she raised the word *stranded*. The next time she came back from a trip, she didn't come back to me.

"Stranded in the Jungle," in its original version(s)—it was written and recorded by the Jayhawks in 1956 and quickly remade into a hit by the Cadets—is a novelty single, a piece of comedy, like "Run, Red, Run" or "Alley Oop." Half of it is told by a man who has been captured by cannibals and whose girlfriend is still at home. In the other half, which takes place "back in the States," the romantic rival of the castaway comes on to his girlfriend. Your man's finished, he tells her, so you might as well choose me. The two halves of the song are played in entirely different styles—the States is slick doo-wop, while the jungle is native-sounding drums, animal noises, and scary booga-booga cannibals: "I smelled something cooking and I looked to see / That's when I found out they was a-cookin' me." (As many people have pointed out, it's not exactly a civil rights anthem, though there's more than a little Frantz Fanon: "The zone where the natives live is not complementary to the zone inhabited by the settlers," etc.) It's a song about opposites that can't be reconciled, but it's also a song about reconciling them. If the Bee Gees' "I've Gotta Get a Message to You" (1968) is one of the scriptural songs about mis- or noncommunication, "Stranded in the Jungle" is another one.

> *I was stranded in the jungle*
> *Afraid and alone*

The man is in hot water with the cannibals, literally and figuratively. They don't seem predisposed to let him go. As long as he is in the jungle, his girlfriend "back in the States" will hear nothing from him, and as long as she hears nothing, she's vulnerable to the advances of his rival. So he does what any man would do: He breaks loose from the cannibals, hitches a ride on a whale, makes it home, and reclaims his lover.

> *Baby, baby, your man is no good*
> *Baby, baby, you should've understood*
> *You can trust me as long as can be*

It's a nice story. Who doesn't like a happy ending? The only worthwhile message is the one you deliver yourself. If you want someone to talk to you (or love you, or trust you), talk to them (or love them, or trust them). Simple. Imagine if the Bee Gees' "I've Gotta Get a Message to You," which has a similarly dire circumstance (melodramatic, not comic, but still), ended this way, with the condemned man hightailing it away from death row. And then imagine that death row and the jungle are metaphors for romantic separation.

As for the song, the Jayhawks' version is harder to find (it's available on an Ace UK import called *The Golden Age of American Rock & Roll, Vol. 5*) and fairly tame. The Cadets' insta-cover is more assured and funnier. As fine as it is, it's blown clear out of the (hot) water by the New York Dolls' version. In David Johansen's hands, and lungs, the jungle is deeper and darker than the Cadets' jungle, and the animal noises sound less like nature and more like the terrifying hoots and howls of uncivilized punks. Which, of course, they are.

SADNESS/HAPPINESS

A SADNESS FOR THINGS
Calvin Scott
Released 1971
Available on: *The Complete Stax / Volt Soul Singles, Vol. 2: 1968–1971*
Stax: 1993

WHAT A SAD FEELING
Betty Harris
Released 1965
Available on: *Soul Perfection Plus*
Westside UK: 1998

SAD OLD WORLD
Frank Black — *Fast Man Raider Man*
Back Porch: 2006

I CAN'T GO TO SLEEP
Wu-Tang Clan (featuring Isaac Hayes) — *The W*
Loud: 2000

WAVES OF FEAR
Lou Reed — *The Blue Mask*
RCA: 1982

A FEW YEARS AGO, I WAS TAKING A TRIP, AND AT SOME POINT ALONG THE way I had a layover in Chicago. For an hour, I sat in the bustle of O'Hare and watched the people pass by, their brows furrowed with one worry or another—maybe the mortgage was late or the insurance on the second car was too expensive or the husband was putting on weight in a way that seemed to indicate depression or the stepson was developing violent tendencies or the boss wasn't showing enough respect or the lover wasn't loving back the way she used to or the mother needed surgery. Every expression, every gesture, seemed to broadcast a particular sadness. I put my earbuds in to block it all out and went to get something to eat.

In one of the restaurants, I got a sandwich, and while I was sitting there eating it, listening to Kanye West's "Monster" (2010), I saw a woman sitting by herself, also eating. It was an airport. People eat alone all the time. There was no reason to make too much of it. And yet, the more I watched her, the more certain I was that she was sad, and not sad in a transitional or instrumental way, but deeply, foundationally, irreversibly sad. She was in her midthirties, attractive but tired-looking, reading a business report filled with black-and-white charts. At one point, she took out her cell phone, started to make a call, and thought better of it. The hand holding the phone sunk down until it was in her lap. I had taken my earbuds out. I put them back in.

That particular time, I went from Chicago to San Francisco. When I got there, I had drinks with a friend of mine. She was flying from Seattle to New York, and happened to be in the airport at the same time. We sat in the airport. We talked about the airport. It was all very airport. Eventually I got around to the woman in the Chicago airport. My friend grew angry. I thought she was angry I was still talking about airports, but she had issues with my analysis. My problem, she said, wasn't that I was assuming that these other people's lives were sad, but that I thought somehow my life was better than theirs. "Well," I said.

I didn't know what I was going to say next. Luckily, she went on. She said that the reason I felt conflicted was that my feelings took the form of pity rather than plain sadness. If I allowed myself to simply feel sad for people, it might lead to sympathy rather than some dumb combination of pain and superiority. We were all in the same boat, so we might as well acknowledge our powerlessness before that fact.

The truth of what she had said lasted for a few minutes. But then parts of her argument started to shimmer, like a mirage, and I wasn't as certain anymore. The part about connecting to the common humanity in us all had a certain appeal, but the part about doing away with the dumb mix of pain and superiority bothered me. Isn't that what much artwork is about? You feel the pain, it starts to drive you to your knees, you bring yourself back up (thanks to a narcissistic impulse), you move forward on this cushion of temporary superiority and use the energy generated by this process to create something from nothing. In fact, after a few times, you come to value the sadness, to receive it with a kind of joy, because you know that it will, in time, bring you to creative work.

Songs about sadness, of course, are highly common. There's the sad-eyed lady and the sad mood, there's fa-fa-fa-fa-fa, there's "Sadly Beautiful" (The Replacements, 1990) and "To Be Young (Is to Be Sad, Is to Be High)" (Ryan Adams, 2000) and "Sad Machine" (Porter Robinson, 2014). But songs about the fact that the world is sad are rarer. Calvin Scott, a blind pianist and singer, was born in 1938 in Alabama and performed with the also-blind Clarence Carter before a car accident ended the duo's career. Carter, of course, went on to have huge hits like "Slip Away" (1968) and "Strokin'" (1988); Scott became a minor soul performer for Atlantic and then Stax, and he released a few singles and an album called *I'm Not Blind . . . I Just Can't See.* "A Sadness for Things" (1971), the lead-off track, moves through an almost comically inclusive litany of sad things ("Intelligent parents that are sometimes completely confused . . . Street dogs and lost kittens and people that cry"). Betty Harris, a New Orleans soul singer best known for her cover of Solomon Burke's "Cry to Me" (1963), returns to the same subject later in "What a Sad Feeling" (1965)—in fact, both she and Scott use dining alone as an archetypal scene of sadness. Maybe they were at O'Hare, too. (Harris employs one of my favorite soul-music tricks: singing about loneliness while a trio of backup singers echoes the sentiment.) Frank Black's "Sad Old World" (2006) exhibits a more minimalist sensibility but also explains how we're wounded by busted love and illness.

I know something about sickness
I know something about that now
There's nothing you can do except witness
No there's nothing you can do
And when the petals on the flower start to curl
Well, you better hang on now

Of course, all this poetry can obscure the fact that sometimes it's impossible to process the world's pain into beautiful sadness. Sometimes existence leaves you raw, at which point sadness (for others) turns to fear (for yourself), which in turn leads to rage and self-loathing and self-medication and sleeplessness and Ghostface and Lou Reed.

GENEROSITY/SELFISHNESS

OH, CANDY
Cheap Trick — *Cheap Trick*
Epic: 1977

LISTEN
Lambchop — *No You Cmon*
Merge: 2004

SYMPATHY
Sleater-Kinney — *One Beat*
Kill Rock Stars: 2002

WALKING AND FALLING
Laurie Anderson — *Big Science*
Warner Bros.: 1982

As these playlists demonstrate, there has been, throughout my life, a certain type of female friend who has come to me with problems. Call it a pattern. When I was very young, these were girls I was interested in dating. Why else would you listen to four thousand hours of someone else's problems? Ha ha. I am joking. Here is an answer to that question: You would listen to someone else's problems because listening to the problems of people you care about is both altruistic and selfish, in that it exhibits kindness and also illuminates aspects of the human condition, which is vital, especially if you plan to be a writer. When I was twenty, I wanted trust and I wanted to trust other people. I was willing to listen. I was not shy about giving advice when I thought it was appropriate. I had a certain appetite for problems and no real capacity for being shocked. And I was interested in seeing if any of the emotional intimacy would spill over into romance. So that was what happened.

Fast-forward fifty years. Now rewind twenty. Now rewind another ten. Now fast-forward five. Okay. That's about right. That's about now. The phenomenon I have sketched above continues to occur, with several key differences. Just this week, for example, I heard some problems from female friends. Two friends, in fact, with two separate sets of problems. Because I have been trusted with these problems, I am obligated to blur the facts, and so I will also furnish some incorrect details. These people are half-Japanese. These people like the band Half Japanese. These people never read magazines, and they once punched a guy in the stomach during a music festival in Portland, Oregon. There. That should do it.

Anyway, this week, these two people had discussions with me about sad things in their lives. One of the women was suffering from romantic problems, the other from a combination of financial and creative difficulties. I tried my best to draw soberly upon my own experiences of tumult and trouble, as well as things I have read. I tried to give good advice. One women was frustrated and kept pounding the table at the coffee shop where we sat. The other cried over the telephone. I didn't mind. That's how it goes. Times get tough. Self-worth wiggles and wobbles. People get sad. They need friends to pick them up. If I had to do it all over again, I might have followed up by e-mailing each of them a copy of "Oh, Candy" (1977), one of the saddest songs ever written about an irretrievably sad friend.

> *Oh, Candy, why did you do it*
> *You didn't stick a needle in your vein*
> *You just got so damned depressed*
> *We all liked you except yourself*

The Candy of the title isn't the Warhol superstar Candy Darling, who died in 1974. Rather, it's Marshall Mintz, a photographer friend of the band, who hanged himself. His nickname came from his initials, MM, or M&M. Rick Nielsen, who wrote the song, changed Mintz's gender to make the song's emotions more universal.

My advice to the two women wasn't as inspirational as "Oh, Candy." It ran more toward hopeful bromides. He's a jerk, I said to one. Money has a way of coming in cycles, I said to the other. In the end, it made them feel better. I know because they told me. And that was my aim, to make them feel better, so far as I could. Job well done. I went home. I ate dinner with my wife and my kids. I shot baskets at the playground with my older son. I thought about how easy it had been to help. All I had to do was listen, which is what Kurt Wagner's doing in "Listen" (2004).

> Tell your trouble to
> Someone stuck here just like you

Then, later that night, what had been easy hardened. I became exhausted. I collapsed on the couch and woke up in the middle of the night with an evil question in my mind. I am not going to disclose the question just yet, because it's embarrassing. Isn't that what writing is for, though, at least in part—to give voice to the thoughts that cross your mind, catch sight of themselves in the mirror, and run off, appalled by their own ugliness? I'll assume it is. So here's the thought I had when I woke in the middle of the night: Where's my goddamn reward? If you spend time being a big fat shoulder for someone to cry on, aren't they supposed to go to the gift store and pick something out and send it to you? Yecch.

Even now, it makes me unhappy to hear myself think that. How bad a person does that thought make me? As bad as Martin Shkreli, the pharmaceutical CEO who overcharged HIV patients for their drugs, conspicuously purchased a bespoke Wu-Tang Clan album for $2 million before being arrested on insider trading charges? As bad as Walter Palmer, the Minneapolis dentist who paid $50,000 to kill a thirteen-year-old protected lion in Zimbabwe? As bad as Jared Fogle? No, not that bad.

What was I? The charitable answer is that it puts me significantly south of any of them, because all I was really doing was desiring, after the fact, in an imprecise way, that the friendship be mutual. But if the charitable answer came so easily, I wouldn't have been grappling with this in the first place.

I couldn't find a song to illustrate this feeling, not exactly, because there's no song called "A Selfish Jackalope." The closest I could come was Sleater-Kinney's "Sympathy" (2002), which isn't about adult friends, men and women, dealing or not dealing with each other. It's about Corin Tucker's fear over having a premature baby and her appeal to God. It would be presumptuous and even idiotic to insert myself into that relationship, even for the purposes of understanding my reaction to the people who need my sympathetic ear, and for that reason I'm going to do it.

> I know I come to you only when in need
> I'm not the best believer, not the most deserving

Do people deserve to be heard when in need? Yes, obviously. Candy did. So did my friends. But what happens when they can't or don't reciprocate? Or, more to the point, when they aren't aware of the ways in which they can? One of the problems with being a good listener or a strong friend is that roles harden. Just because I don't say I'm not sad doesn't mean I'm not sometimes. Just because I don't ask for help doesn't mean I couldn't use it. I guess I could say, "Hey, look, I am always happy to listen to you, but yesterday I got this crazy fleeting sense that I want you to be a better listener. It landed on me like a black butterfly while I was sleeping. Then it spoke and said, 'Remind them that they have the power to comfort you, too.' At any rate, forget it, because that fleeting sense has fled. I am mortified. Back to normal."

I would never say that.

I got older. Time passed. I got wiser after even more time passed. Eventually, I worked up the courage to articulate this idea to one of my friends. She had an interesting response. "What reward do you want?" she said. The question deafened me. What reward would I want? Money? Dirty pictures? Whiskey? An e-card? A hug? A puppy? For everyone to be twenty again, filled with possibility, roles not yet clearly defined? I guess the sane, safe answer is that I want to trust that friends know to what the question pertains, and that they'll be mindful to pick the appropriate reward and deliver it at the appropriate time. That sounds like a dodge. In fact, it's both a cop-out and an opt-in. Which is, maybe, what friendship has to be to be real. I think of the poignant search that opens Laurie Anderson's "Walking and Falling" (1982): "I wanted you and I was looking for you, but I couldn't find you." Join the club. It meets regularly, but we can't say where.

FEAR/BRAVERY

BRAVE AND STRONG
Sly and the Family Stone — *There's a Riot Goin' On*
Epic: 1971

I'M NOT AFRAID TO DIE
Gillian Welch — *Hell Among the Yearlings*
Acony: 1998

NOT AFRAID
Bizzy Bone — *Alpha and Omega*
Bungalo: 2004

JEANNIE'S AFRAID OF THE DARK
Robbie Fulks — *13 Hillbilly Giants*
Bloodshot: 2001

IS IT SCARY
Michael Jackson — *Blood On The Dance Floor: HIStory in the Mix*
Epic: 1997

THE FEAR
Pulp — *This Is Hardcore*
Island: 1998

"I'm afraid," she said. "Deathly afraid." Another time, she said, "I'm afraid of death." She was twenty-two. I was a little younger. We had nothing to fear, as it turned out. But it was a summer after college, and we were reading lots of philosophy. Maybe that was what caused the trouble. She was small, brunette, smarter than she gave herself credit for being—and she gave herself a tremendous amount of credit. When we broke up, after about six months, her fear still had a hold over her. "I'm scared of what will happen now," she said, and we briefly got back together. But she also said, "I'm scared to stay here knowing what else is out there," which led to the second and final breakup. It was how she spoke, how she thought, how she was: always with the fear. When I was with her, I started to informally collect songs about fear. I was afraid I wouldn't find any, but as it turns out, pop music is full of fear: John Cale's *Fear*, Public Enemy's *Fear of a Black Planet*, Talking Heads' *Fear of Music*. Even songs that say they're about bravery, like Sly and the Family Stone's "Brave and Strong" (1971), are also about the absence of bravery.

> *Frightened faces to the wall*
> *Can't you hear your mama call?*
> *The brave and strong survive*

What are they surviving? What are the types of fear that turn the faces to the wall? The big fear that hangs over all the others, of course, is the fear of death. I recently passed through a period where it seemed to be everywhere. My wife was commemorating the anniversary of her mother's death and worrying about her father. A friend in her twenties was taken to the hospital, unexpectedly, for something that turned out to be nothing but had her family worried, briefly, that it might be everything. Another friend in her thirties told me matter-of-factly that she has been thinking of dying often. Or rather, thinking of dying once, often.

In all of these cases, I tried to put this fear to rest. I told my wife that her father seemed healthy enough—absurdly healthy for a man in his nineties, in fact—but that there's nothing that can be done to keep out the Uninvited Guest. I sent cheery messages to my twentysomething friend. I told my thirtysomething friend that she can think of dying all she wants, so long as she's not afraid of it. "Being too afraid can interfere with your life," I said. She said nothing. Her silence was more eloquent than my words. There are songs that also have something to say about this issue. In "I'm Not Afraid to Die" (1998), Gillian Welch finds solace in the inevitable.

Forget my sins upon the wind
My hobo soul will rise

Bizzy Bone's "Not Afraid" (2004) takes a less lyrical route to the same destination.

I'm not afraid to die
I'm not afraid to fight
And we can bang bang all day, all night
This is how we ride

So two versions, one peaceful, one violent. What is there to fear? According to my thirtysomething friend: being alone on your deathbed, with no company, no family, no solace. Oh, and not having any confidence that you'll go on to something better. Fear under those conditions seems like the only rational response.

It's strange that fear of death makes people feel so alone, because it's something shared by almost everyone. "Jeannie's Afraid of the Dark" is one of the eerier songs on the Dolly Parton–Porter Wagoner duet album *Just the Two of Us*, from 1968. (The version I know better is a fairly faithful Robbie Fulks cover from 2001 that preserves the almost unbearable five-hankie weepiness of the thing.) Jeannie's a little girl, afraid of the dark, and every night she runs to her parents' room so that she doesn't have to sleep alone. One day, her parents take her to the cemetery, and she makes a morbid (not to mention unhygienic) request—that when she die she not be buried, because she won't be able to deal with the dark. Jeannie might have benefited from Paul Tillich's *The Courage to Be*, which was still a relatively recent publication (sixteen years old) when the original Dolly-Porter song came out. Here's what Tillich writes:

> The first assertion about the nature of anxiety is this: anxi-
> ety is the state in which a being is aware of its possible
> nonbeing. The same statement, in a shorter form, would
> read: anxiety is the existential awareness of nonbeing . . .
> It is not the realization of universal transitoriness, not even
> the experience of the death of others, but the impression
> of these events on the always latent awareness of our own
> having to die that produces anxiety.

So how to deal with these anxieties? Well, one way, weirdly, is to feel fear—fear, that is, of other things, things that don't involve annihilation. In fact, other fears are life-affirming, because they require being. So be afraid of snakes. Be afraid of clowns. Be afraid of ghosts. (That's why fear of the dark has a special status, I think—it's easy to forget that you exist.)

The other night I was talking to a friend whose husband is a film scholar specializing in horror. I was asking what counts as the minimum requirement for a horror movie, as opposed to a scary movie. Does someone have to die? Does more than half of the audience have to scream? Does the film have to be aware of the entertainment value of its own capacity for producing fear? "There are books written about that," she said. And, I imagine, about the masturbatory subtext of werewolf movies and the STD subtext metaphors of vampire movies, sure, but what did she think? She wouldn't say.

I brought the question with me back to music. What's scary? Fantômas? Scott Walker? Nico? Is bleakness scary? Is brilliant rage like Ice Cube scary? Is rueful truth like Gil Scott-Heron scary? Is experimental creepiness like the Residents scary? And if those songs are scary, what's a horror song? I found two, I think: Michael Jackson's "Is It Scary" (1997), which is an unholier-than-"Thriller" piece of meta-horror in which he keeps testing your threshold for experiencing terror as entertainment ("There's a creak beneath the floor / There's a creak behind the door"), and Pulp's "The Fear" (1998), which does more or less the same thing, stacking misgivings like bricks in English bond ("Here comes the fear again / The end is near again"). The effects in both songs are so outsized, so preposterous, that they shouldn't work at all, and yet both of them work frightfully well at delivering their messages. Existence may be terrible and scary, but it's life. It goes and goes again. And it has death beat by a mile.

ONE/NONE

I'M THE ONE
Descendents — *Everything Sucks*
Epitaph: 1996

YOU'RE THE ONE
Paul Simon — *You're the One*
Warner Bros.: 2000

I'M THE ONE
Van Halen — *Van Halen*
Warner Bros.: 1978

YOU'RE THE ONE (PARTS 1 & 2)
Little Sister — Single
Stone Flower: 1970

I'M ONE
The Who — *Quadrophenia*
Track: 1973

YEARS AGO, I WENT TO AN ART OPENING IN MIAMI. IT WAS A HOT NIGHT, and half the people in the gallery seemed like they just wanted to get off the street. I had been looking at the paintings in the exhibit. Some were abstracts. Some were portraits painted from newspaper photographs. I told a woman nearby that I liked them. She was extremely pretty, with a flip of blond hair and large, dark eyes.

"Made 'em," she said. She had one of the original newspaper photographs with her as proof. On the back there was an ad for a restaurant. I took her to dinner there on what I thought was a date; she politely disagreed after dessert and a drink by removing my hand from her leg. We became friends. We became close. I hung out in her apartment, which doubled as her studio, and talked about everything: politics, books, songs, sex, travel, drugs, dogs, outer space. Then one afternoon she went out to put gas in her car, and I was left alone with her paintings. They were the canvases I had thought of as abstract, but I realized with horror that they were no such thing. They were portraits of men, mostly nude, viewed at extremely close range. Once you saw them in that light you could make out a stubbled cheek or a muscular leg, or worse.

I didn't say anything to her about them, but I did say something to another friend of mine. "It's creepy," I said. "There are so many of them and only one of me."

"But what do you care? You're not dating her."

"Neither are they," I said. "But they're crowding me out."

"On the other hand," she said, "there's only one of you, and the rest of them are nowhere to be found. Maybe that means you're winning."

It was an interesting idea. Like most interesting ideas, it was at least half-wrong. I wasn't winning anything. I was spending time in the company of someone else's talent and beauty. The second fact sometimes made the first fact weak in the knees. I was a young man then. I felt the situation was profoundly unfair. I obsessed about what she did when she wasn't spending her time with me. The obsession caused me some distress. I am pleased to report that it has, over the years, become extremely easy to laugh at the moony preoccupations of my younger self. Back then, though, I self-medicated with bad moods and good music. One of the songs I listened to as painkiller was the Descendents' "I'm the One" (1996). It had punch, in the sense that it had both power and aim.

> *I'm the one*
> *Whose shoulder you've been cryin' on*
> *Nice guys finish last*
> *No one knows as good as me*

At some point, we fought, this woman and me. I think that I slipped up and confessed my feelings. She told me that I couldn't stay in her studio when she wasn't there. "I came here once and you were sleeping on the couch," she said, which wasn't true at all. I was only pretending to sleep.

I returned morosely to the friend who had told me not to worry about the paintings of the nude men. "It's not like you were the one and now you're a zero," she said. "You're still the one. You're just the one who made her unhappy instead of the one who made her happy." I was beginning to sense that my friend was a disordered optimist. Still, the insight wasn't hers alone. Paul Simon struck the same note a few years later in "You're the One" (2000), the title track to an underpowered but lovely album.

> You're the one
> You broke my heart
> You made me cry

Later, because he's Paul Simon and intelligent analysis of emotional states is one of his principal traits, he sets down his guitar and takes a short walk around the lyric so that he can see things from the reverse view.

> When I hear it from the other side
> It's a completely different song
> I'm the one who made you cry
> And I'm the one who's wrong

The song fades out with the two parties taking turns being the one, both for painful and pleasurable purposes. By the time I heard that song, I was no longer friends with any of the people in this story. They are all distant memories, though not so distant that I doubt they once existed. As you get older, you're supposed to worry less about awkward moments of emotional uncertainty. The relationships you forge come to strengthen you. Marriage and parenthood become sites of renewable nourishment. Friendships can then be allowed to proceed through various phases, bending but never breaking.

But very young men don't know any of this. Here I will cite the work of the American poet David Lee Roth (born 1954, Bloomington, Indiana). I should start by saying that the Van Halen / Van Hagar question is not much of a question. "Panama" (1983) is the best song ever written about a new car sung by a guy who sounds like he's trying to sell you a used car. "I'm the One" might not even be one of Diamond Dave's top ten performances. Still, it has always been one of my favorite Van Halen songs, a great piece of expressive comedy and also a surprisingly sly boast/plea from the band to its fans. It takes the idea of being the one and diffuses it—he's not the one to another known one, but rather to thousands of potential ones.

> Look at all these little kids
> Takin' care of the music biz
> Don't their business take good care of me?
> Honey! I'm the one, the one you love

The song that sits on the other side of the seesaw here is Little Sister's "You're the One" (1970). Produced by Sly Stone, with a Sly Stone bass line, a Sly Stone guitar part, Sly Stone–arranged horns, and a brilliant but infuriating Sly Stone lyric, "You're the One" stretches out the notion of ego even further. In it, not only do you not need another person to feel good, but you don't need another person to feel bad.

> I'm the one my life has taught to fight
> To turn around would never make it right
> Inside out or outside in
> The way you go depends on where you've been

The lyric doesn't exactly make sense, which makes me suspect that it's deeply and irrefutably true. Message to Sly: You can throw rocks or you can throw rice, 'cause paradox is paradise.

When it comes to questions of feeling special, and songs that question what you do in the moments when you don't feel special, the inevitable destination is the Who's "I'm One" (1973), one of rock and roll's most eloquent and moving statements on adolescent alienation.

> *Every year is the same and I feel it again*
> *I'm a loser—no chance to win*
> *Leaves start falling, come down is calling*
> *Loneliness starts sinking in*

I've seen the band play the song loud and I've seen Pete Townshend, solo, perform it as an intimate sing-along. You'd think that the warm embrace of a crowd would tarnish the song's message of defiant solitude, but it just seemed to polish it up. Truly great songs are invulnerable. And this is one.

OPTIMISM/PESSIMISM

END OF THE RAINBOW
Sonny and Linda Sharrock — *Paradise*
ATCO: 1975

END OF THE RAINBOW
Elvis Costello
Released 1985
King of America (expanded edition)
Rhino: 2005

RAINBOW
Gene Chandler
Released 1962
Available on: *Vee-Jay: The Definitive Collection*
Shout! Factory: 2007

RAINBOW '65
Gene Chandler
Released 1965
Available on: *Beg, Scream & Shout: The Big Ol' Box of Sixties Soul*
Rhino: 1997

OVER THE RAINBOW
Jerry Lee Lewis
Released 1980
Available on: *The Jerry Lee Lewis Anthology—All Killer No Filler!*
Rhino: 1993

GOD PUT A RAINBOW IN THE SKY
Mahalia Jackson
Released 1959
Available on: *Gospels, Spirituals & Hymns*
Columbia Legacy: 1991

I can't say I don't like Radiohead. I once loved *The Bends*; when it was released I nearly wore out the cassette listening to "High and Dry" (1995). But I wasn't able to get fully behind the albums after that—not *OK Computer* (I tried and failed), not *Hail to the Thief* (the packaging excited me, the record less so). But when, in the heady and experimental days of 2007, the band announced that it was releasing a new record, *In Rainbows*, for download at whatever price customers wished, I snapped it up instantly. It wasn't because it was cheap. It was because of the title.

Years later, it's the one thing that still sticks with me. I played the record recently so I could look at the cover image. It suggested something trippy, emotional, and colorful. It suggested more than that. It suggested a memory. When I first downloaded *In Rainbows*, when I first listened to it, I dozed off a bit. As I say, I wasn't able to fully get behind Radiohead. But as I dozed, I had a vivid dream of driving with a girlfriend in northern Indiana in 1994. At the time, we were living together on the near north side of Chicago and both going to graduate school; I was at Northwestern and she was at the School of the Art Institute. After she finished her program, she got a job teaching painting on Saturdays in South Bend. I drove her down each week and hung around while she taught. Then we got lunch and drove back to Chicago. It was tiring, but it wasn't awful.

And then at some point it *was* awful. We had gotten together young—I was barely twenty, and she was a few years older—and the kinds of fears and ambitions that we might have been able to survive a decade later consumed us. She passed through periods of depression. I passed through periods of nonspecific fury. The relationship melted like a wax face near an open flame. With our luck gone, it became a matter of will, and I'm not sure that either of us wanted things to improve. At some point, all the backing and forthing started to shake the frame of our feelings for each other. By the time I drove her out to South Bend, it was already too late, even though I did not realize it at the time. (Once, on the drive, one of us comically started calling South Bend "the Bend," though this was about two years before *The Bends* came out. That happened in real life and it happened again in the dream. It's irrelevant, unless it's a mystical point of contact.)

The class lasted about eight weekends. On one of the last Saturdays, we were driving home, endless fields on our sides, and we saw a rainbow in the sky. It was like something a child would draw, with clearly defined bands of color and a perfect arc. And it was huge. I don't know how rainbows are actually measured, but this was larger than any rainbow I had ever seen. I joked that maybe it was the result of an industrial accident in Gary. She didn't laugh at my joke, but she marveled at the rainbow with me. We kept driving. When the road curved away to the north, I tried to keep the rainbow in the corner of my eye, but at some point I lost it and when I turned to look, it was gone. About a month later, I went to visit my parents, and when I came back, she had moved out of our apartment.

We had marveled at the rainbow together. We had experienced its disappearance together. That was our relationship, writ small. When I dreamed about the rainbow, I was dreaming about the relationship. When I woke remembering it, I was remembering the relationship. Rainbows have baffled people for as long as there have been people. The ancient Greeks thought that rainbows were the contrails of gods, traces of their paths as they left earth for the heavens. The Hindu believe that rainbows were actual bows, and that thunder and lightning are arrows fired from them. The Irish, at least in cereal commercials, think that a rainbow can be a kind of treasure map. Find the end, and you'll find a pot of gold, like the wordless, beautiful "End of the Rainbow" (1975) by Sonny Sharrock and then-wife Linda.

If rainbows are mysterious, they are, in that regard, like relationships. Maybe that's why one brought me to the other. They—rainbows and relationships both—are highly equivocal phenomena, sources of intense optimism and intense pessimism at once. One of the most persuasive arguments regarding the dark side of rainbows is made by

Richard Thompson in "The End of the Rainbow" (1974), from *I Want to See the Bright Lights Tonight*. Thompson is no stranger to depressing lyrics, but these take the cake, douse it in cheap wine, and leave it in the alley to rot. Elvis Costello covered the song during the *King of America* sessions (1985), and kept in most of the anguish.

> *I feel for you, you little horror*
> *Safe at your mother's breast*
> *No lucky break for you around the corner*

The family situation is poor ("your father is a bully," "your sister she's no better than a whore"), and it doesn't seem to be improving. And the overall situation it's pointing to is philosophically, terminally bleak.

> *Life seems so rosy in the cradle*
> *But I'll be a friend, I'll tell you what's in store*
> *There's nothing at the end of the rainbow*
> *There's nothing to grow up for anymore*

Here, the rainbow is false hope, and its promise of reward is a cruel trick. Recently, a friend of mine started a relationship. "Everything is brighter," she said. "I mean things like colors. Remember a week ago when I was having a terrible day and everything seemed gray? This is different." That's the rainbow. Without it, there's just daytime: one colorless stream of light that isn't ramified into passionate reds and yellows and indigos. The rainbow gives you color, but does it support your weight?

One of the most complicated uses of the metaphor comes in Gene Chandler's "Rainbow" (1962), a landmark of Chicago soul that was co-written with Curtis Mayfield. First, Chandler says that he has a rainbow in his heart, which seems nice until he reveals that the rainbow reminds him of how he and his girlfriend parted. She's "gone forever," as it turns out, but he's not the kind of guy to back down from a challenge: "deep down in my heart," he pledges, he'll "love her forever." What permits him this forbearance? Is it the rainbow? Does it function as a source of optimism? And if so, is it real or false? The song was rerecorded by Chandler several times; the 1965 version has a full gospel-soul breakdown where he admits how painful it is to carry around a good feeling about a bad situation.

> *I'm down on my knees, please listen to my plea*
> *I'm looking up above, pray for your love*
> *Please, please stop this rainbow*

When I was driving with my girlfriend and saw the rainbow in the sky, I saw it as a symbol of hope. Not all of the rainbow is the end.

If you don't want the rainbow to end, you have a few options. The most obvious is to keep going beyond it, as explained in Harold Arlen and E. Y. Harburg's "Over the Rainbow," which was written for Judy Garland's starring role in *The Wizard of Oz* in 1939 and almost immediately became an American standard. Garland probably sang it so many times that *bluebird* and *lullaby* started to sound like nonsense words to her, and it's been covered by hundreds of other singers. For me, the best version is by Jerry Lee Lewis (1980). It starts with a cloppety-clop saloon piano figure and quickly turns into unholy gospel. People talk all kinds of nonsense about phrasing, but listen to how Jerry Lee sings the lyric "where kisses are melting like lemon drops." Or the other lyrics: "that's where they'll find me," or the strange moment of personalization, "ol' Jerry Lee." Or, for that matter, how he plays the piano.

If you don't go over the rainbow, you can get under it. Mahalia Jackson's "God Put a Rainbow in the Sky" (1959) isn't her only rainbow song—three years earlier, she had recorded the more didactic "There Is No Color Line 'Round the Rainbow"—but it's her best, reaching back into the Bible and also up into the heavens.

When God shut Noah in the grand old ark
God put a rainbow in the sky
Oh, yes, the sun grew dim and the days were dark
God put a rainbow in the sky

Most of the song, of course, is just Mahalia wailing, testifying, calling on the children to hear her testify. It pays to reprint the lyrics, if only to demonstrate the power of song over words; reading them is like looking at the names of colors instead of at the colors themselves.

God put a rainbow in the sky
A rainbow in the sky
A rainbow in the sky
Oh, God put a rainbow in the sky

Apart from the brilliant mispronunciation in the chorus—Jackson sometimes says "rainboat" instead of "rainbow," maybe to remind us about the ark—the song is a straightforward and undeniable reminder about what rainbows really are. They are the opportunity for happiness, but not without a tinge of the sadness that is required to produce it. They are simultaneously the signal that the storm has broken and the reminder of the storm. I'm not sure why there was one off the road in Indiana. Given what eventually happened, there shouldn't have been.

STUFF/UNSTUFF

LOW YO YO STUFF
Captain Beefheart and the Magic Band
Released 1972
Available on: *The Spotlight Kid / Clear Spot*
Reprise: 1999

HOT STUFF
The Rolling Stones — *Black and Blue*
Rolling Stones: 1976

YOU THINK YOU'RE HOT STUFF
Jean Knight
Released 1971
Available on: *Mr. Big Stuff* (expanded edition)
Stax: 1990

SISTER BIG STUFF
John Holt
Released 1973
Available on: *One Thousand Volts of Holt* (expanded edition)
Sanctuary Trojan: 2002

COME AND GET THIS STUFF
Syreeta — *Stevie Wonder Presents Syreeta*
Motown: 1974

STUFFS AND THINGS
Funkadelic — *Let's Take It to the Stage*
20th Century / Westbound: 1975

A TALL WOMAN I KNOW DATED A TALL FRIEND OF MINE, BRIEFLY, AND then, after breaking up with him, became friends with me and my wife. Her height is not an issue except in the sense that it is the only way anyone ever identifies her. "Your tall friend," they say. She was over at the house recently. We were drinking some wine she brought. "What kind of wine is this?" I said. "Red, I guess?" she said. We were most of the way through the bottle. As she opened a second bottle, one of the three of us raised the issue of pleasure, and specifically about the differences between childhood pleasures and adulthood pleasures. Our friend was wondering why, when, and how the things that excited her as a child (cartoons, games, new streets, new jokes) gave way to adult opiates: money, alcohol, and especially sex. The stuff she did as a kid wasn't the same stuff she's doing as an adult; the adult stuff was more limited, more narrow, although arguably more powerful. It's an e pluribus unum situation: Out of many childhood pleasures come a few adult pleasures, and possibly only one. The word *stuff* seemed okay as a placeholder at first, but as time went on it started to settle in, partly because of its connotations of filling and being filled, and partly because it's the centerpiece of many songs.

Take Captain Beefheart's "Low Yo Yo Stuff" (1972).

> *Now, baby, it's in your being*
> *Whether you're long, tall, short, or skinny*
> *Sometimes it's rough*
> *You mean to tell me it's that Low Yo Yo Stuff?*

What's that stuff? Is it possible that he's activating the pleasures of childhood? Maybe he's playing cards on the road. Maybe he's spinning around until he gets dizzy. But later on, he clarifies.

> *What if my girlfriend back home*
> *Finds out what my fingers have been doing*
> *On my guitar since I been gone?*
> *Don't anybody tell her*
> *I been doing the Low Yo Yo Yo Yo*
> *Like any other fella*

As Captain Beefheart songs go, this one is fairly straightforward, both lyrically and musically. It's closer to "Shake Your Booty" or "Rump Shaker" or "Dancing in the Sheets" than it is to "Sweet Sweet Bulbs." It could be a Rolling Stones song. In fact, the opening riff sounds similar to the Stones' "Hey Negrita," from the 1976 album *Black and Blue*. Mick Taylor had recently departed, and the Stones were trying out a set of new guitarists. Ron Wood, who would eventually be selected to replace Taylor, played lead on "Hey Negrita," but the most surprising song on the record was "Hot Stuff," a disco song with lead by Harvey Mandel, the blues-rock guitarist who had previously played with Charlie Musselwhite and Canned Heat. Here, there's a bit more equivocation with the "stuff": For most of the lyric, it seems to be music itself, or a general expression of the exhilaration that accompanies playing it. It's self-referential. Only in the last two verses does it begin to dovetail with Beefheart's stuff. And, of course, because this is the Stones—and especially because this is *Black and Blue*—the last verse reminds us which people have the hottest stuff. Here's a hint: not white European people.

> *To everybody in Jamaica*
> *That's working in the sun*
> *Your hot, your hot stuff*
> *Shake it up, hot stuff*

The phrase had been around for a while. Vess Ossman recorded the ragtime hit "Hot Stuff Patrol" in 1897. But the sexual implication became increasingly explicit. By the time of Donna Summer's megahit three years after *Black and Blue*, there was no doubt what it meant. That song's not here. Neither is "Mr. Big Stuff," the megahit released five years before *Black and Blue*, on which Jean Knight, a New Orleans soul singer recording for Stax, stood her ground against a ladies' man. Here, the stuff in question is male stuff, and it's sizable, related to his money and his "fancy clothes" and his "big fine car." Many girls have fallen for it, but Knight resists.

Later in 1971, she released a sequel to the song, "You Think You're Hot Stuff," that plowed the same furrow with less yield. (There are a dozen other Big Stuff offshoots, at least. Here's one: "Sister Big Stuff" from 1973 by the late reggae legend John Holt, who stuffed the Stones' Jamaican stuff and Knight's big stuff into the same casing.) In "You Think You're Hot Stuff," Knight, aware of adult pleasures but also the risk of suffering emotional pain in the course of pursuing them, tells Mr. Big Stuff he'll never get her stuff (though she euphemistically calls it her "love"). People aren't always so withholding. Syreeta Wright, singing a lyric that's as lubricious as any Stevie Wonder ever wrote, swoops and chirps while the backup singers coo, "I'm coming, I'm coming, I'm coming, come and get it."

When I had collected all the songs, I sent a list to the tall friend. I figured that it would help answer the question of why the entire kaleidoscope of childhood pleasures gets funneled into a single (admittedly great) adult activity. "No," she said. "I had it the other way around. I said that the pleasures were about getting unstuffed."

"Are you sure?"

"Of course," she said. "My theory was that when you're a kid, it's so easy to see the world as boundless, and when you're an adult, it gets harder, more cluttered, more pressured. The goal was to get unstuffed, which is about being unburdened and liberated. I'm annoyed that you would get it backward."

I remembered that it was her idea, and I agreed that she would know. She was right. Then I listened to Funkadelic's graffilthy "Stuffs and Things" (1975), which says plenty about being liberated, and realized she was wrong.

I'm gonna stuff your stuff with thang
Until I make your whole thang twang
I'm going to do things to your stuff

In 2016, "Uptown Funk," the ubiquitous party-funk anthem by Mark Ronson, featuring Bruno Mars, won the Grammy for Best Song. Ronson, accepting the award, pointed out George Clinton in the audience, recognizing Clinton for inspiring several generations of funk performers. Clinton waved back. Ronson's speech ended, but its implication didn't: Without Clinton, very few bands would have learned the secrets of making that whole thang twang.

14

SENSE/NONSENSE

IF YOU PICK HER TOO HARD (SHE COMES OUT OF TUNE)
Little Richard
Recorded 1972
Available on: *King of Rock and Roll: The Complete Reprise Sessions*
Rhino Handmade: 2005

WE'RE GONNA HAVE A REAL GOOD TIME TOGETHER
The Velvet Underground
Recorded 1969
Available on: *1969: Velvet Underground Live with Lou Reed*
Mercury: 1974

TOO MARVELOUS FOR WORDS
Frank Sinatra — *Songs for Swingin' Lovers!*
Capitol: 1956

TOO MARVELOUS FOR WORDS
Art Tatum
Recorded 1953
The Tatum Solo Masterpieces, Vol. 1
Pablo: 1975

YOU CAN HAVE WATERGATE JUST GIMME SOME BUCKS AND I'LL BE STRAIGHT
The J.B.'s
Released 1973
Available on: *Funky Good Time: The Anthology*
Polydor: 1995

MY BROTHER ONCE WENT ON A TRIP TO VISIT A GIRL HE WAS DATING. He came home. We spoke a few days later. I'm sure that the thing I was supposed to do was to say, "Welcome back" or "How was your trip?" and then leave it at that. But you know how it is with brothers—they're not acquaintances. So we got into a discussion about life and what it means. At some point, philosophy slid into soap opera. He wanted to talk about the relationship he was in, and I was reluctant at first because I didn't think it was a wise idea. The relationship, I mean, not the talking about it, although it turned out that the talking about it wasn't such a great idea, either, because what I said caused additional tension.

What I said was that the relationship seemed to have an element of opportunism. The woman he was seeing seemed to me to be spending time with him under somewhat false pretenses, not in a malicious way but not in an especially provident way, either. I recognized that it was condescending to suggest he wasn't capable of seeing that on his own, or at least making his own determination about how much the false pretenses were offset by genuine feelings. "Forget it," I said. I meant it. I more than meant it. Opening up my mouth suddenly seemed like a big mistake. "Gotta go," I said. I was angry at myself—I should have laid out and said nothing—and then I was angry at language.

Why was I mad at language? Well, let me explain, using more of it. Language has limits, particularly when it is charged with expressing complex emotions. Or rather: There may not be any theoretical limits, but there are operational limits. The operators of the language (in this case, me) are hobbled by conflicts of interest, by positionality and personality, by temerity and timidity. There were no words, or there weren't enough words, or there were too many words that got in the way. Stupid language.

Songs seemed like the better way to go. They have one foot in language, but that foot is tapping. They have meaning but also the spell of melody and the force of rhythm, which improves their ability to address situations that touch on emotional and physical issues along with intellectual ones. This is a contentious stance—again, stupid language—until it's demonstrated. Exhibit A: Little Richard. In the early seventies, Little Richard, like many iconic artists from the fifties, was in limbo, uncertain how to respond to the quickly changing times. The electric blues giants who were still alive released heavy blues-rock records with psychedelic flourishes (Muddy Waters had *Electric Mud*, Howlin'

Wolf had *The Howlin' Wolf Album*), but the rockers faced equally severe identity crises. Each of them dealt with it idiosyncratically, sometimes desperately, and not always to their critical or commercial advantage. Elvis had been to Memphis and was already slouching toward Vegas. Jerry Lee Lewis had shifted over into country. Chuck Berry experienced a Pyrrhic victory when "My Ding-a-Ling" (1972), the worst song he ever recorded, hit number one. Bo Diddley soldiered on at Chess, covering many of the artists who had imitated him. The remaining giant of fifties rock, Little Richard, signed to Reprise and recorded a quartet of records: *The Rill Thing* (1970), *The King of Rock and Roll* (1971), *The Second Coming* (1972), and *Southern Child* (1972). They were roots records, reaching back into country and jazz as well as taking a stab at the rock and roll of the time. His vocals weren't as volcanic as the Specialty sides, but they were more than just respectable, and the songwriting was sometimes fascinatingly personal.

Respectable and fascinating sold poorly. Sales were so sluggish that the fourth album of the series, *Southern Child*, wasn't even released at the time, and only saw the light of day thanks to bootleggers and, eventually, a Rhino anthology of the Reprise years. *Southern Child* is of a piece with the others, with some key differences: more original songs, subtler vocals, and a more mellow feel. It also contains Little Richard's midcareer masterpiece, a country-folk composition called "If You Pick Her Too Hard (She Comes Out of Tune)" (1972). The song has many assets (arresting title, peaceful acoustic guitars, unorthodox structure), but its real strength is in its wordless opening, which consists of some two dozen sweet exhales and then a rousing cry that communicates some kind (and maybe all kinds) of freedom.

> *Ha ha ha ha ha ha ha ha ha ha ha ha ha ha*
> *Whoa whoa whoa yeah yeah yeah*

The *ha*s aren't laughter. The *whoa*s aren't a plea for a horse to stop. They're both expressions of emotion that Little Richard has decided can't be effectively communicated with words. The song has other lyrics, and they're not bad.

> *The sound of your breath mixing with my breath*
> *It's the only sound that's true*
> *The touch of your back pressing on my back*
> *Gives us both a place to play out back*

If you subtract the sexual implications (which make up about 50 percent of the song) and the strangeness of Little Richard addressing a love song to what seems to be a woman (40 percent), there's not much left over, but what there is conveys a simple message: Don't pressure your intimates lest you throw your relationships with them into crisis. It seemed like a good lesson regarding the benefits of laying out rather than charging ahead. And while the song isn't expressly about using language injudiciously, the argument is elevated, and maybe even made true, by the nonsense syllables in the lyrics.

I didn't call my brother to apologize. The timing seemed wrong. Instead, I turned to another song that turns on wordlessness, the Velvet Underground's "We're Gonna Have a Real Good Time Together" (1969). The lyrics aren't artful or even anthemic, but they're not exactly placeholders either.

> *We're gonna laugh and dance and shout together*
> *Na na na na na na na na na na na hey hey hey baby*

Listening to it restored my hope. So now I had two song-messages, one about my understanding that I should have backed off and the other about my hope that good faith would return intact, and they said what they needed to say without any words at all. "Whoa whoa whoa yeah yeah yeah," "na na na na na na na na na na na hey hey hey baby."

Little Richard and Lou Reed weren't the first songwriters to recognize that the language they depended upon for their livelihood was iffy at best. The great Johnny Mercer, who once dismissed a musical he didn't care for by saying "I could eat alphabet soup and shit better lyrics," copped to the problem in 1937, when he fit words to music by Richard Whiting for the film *Ready, Willing, and Able*.

> *You're much too much, and just too very very*
> *To ever be in Webster's dictionary*
> *And so I'm borrowing a love song from the birds*
> *To tell you that you're marvelous*

The song, which was named after the last line, "Too Marvelous for Words," became a standard. Everyone recorded it: Ella Fitzgerald, Billie Holiday, Rosemary Clooney, Nat King Cole, Johnnie Ray, Frankie Laine. In 1947, a version by Jo Stafford was used in the film *Dark Passage*, which starred Humphrey Bogart and Lauren Bacall, and the film also incorporated an instrumental version. The irony of stripping "Too Marvelous for Words" of its marvelous words was not confined to the film. Art Tatum recorded a coruscating solo piano version of the song (as wordless pieces go, it's pretty wordy—all those notes!), and the song even supplied the title of James Lester's biography of Tatum. "Too Marvelous for Words" is about love, of course, but love is just one of many possible sites of failure for language; pretty much any emotion that requires explanation also thwarts explanation.

When I spoke to my brother a few days later, I didn't plan on raising the issue of his girlfriend. He raised it. He said that he had thought more about the situation and why he was in it. He then explained himself poorly. "Things will either get better or they will get worse, and when it's better or worse, then I'll know which way it's going," he said. He was trying to tell me something, and probably trying to tell himself something, but he ran afoul of language. Then, that night, I was listening to the J.B.'s perform "You Can Have Watergate Just Gimme Some Bucks and I'll Be Straight" (1973). The lyrics are largely the title, repeated over and over again, along with a few other short chants and some James Brown punctuation. The song is officially listed as an instrumental, but in this case the small amount of language does everything it needs to do.

> *You can have Watergate*
> *But give me some bucks and I'll be straight: I need some*
> *money*

You can spend all your time discussing the large issues of corruption in society or the complexities of an imperfect relationship, but when it comes down to it, people have needs that have nothing to do with fine-grained discussion, precise rendering of interior states, or persuasive argument. Those things are luxuries. My brother just wanted his bucks and he'd be straight. I was going to call him and recommend the song. But then I'd have to explain the connection, and maybe who the J.B.'s were, and that would mean more words, and maybe picking too hard. I remembered that Little Richard had said, "Whoa whoa whoa yeah yeah yeah," and also something else that he said. He said, "Shut up!" That was good enough for me.

ARTICULATION/
INARTICULATION

WORDS DISOBEY ME
The Pop Group — *Y*
Radarscope/WEA: 1979

IN OTHER WORDS
Sly and the Family Stone
Demo recorded 1982
Available on: *Who in the Funk Do You Think You Are: The Warner Bros. Recordings*
Rhino Handmade: 2001

LANGUAGE IS A VIRUS
Laurie Anderson — *Home of the Brave*
Warner Bros.: 1986

WHEN THE WORDS FROM YOUR HEART GET CAUGHT UP IN YOUR THROAT
Smokey Robinson and the Miracles
Released 1968
Available on: *The Complete Motown Singles Vol. 8: 1968*
Hip-O-Select: 2007

THE LOVE I SAW IN YOU WAS JUST A MIRAGE
Smokey Robinson and the Miracles
Released 1967
Available on: *The Ultimate Collection*
Motown: 1998

FLY ME TO THE MOON (IN OTHER WORDS)
Smokey Robinson — *Timeless Love*
New Door: 2006

I HAVE JUST FINISHED WRITING ABOUT THE LIMITS OF LANGUAGE, THE way that our most complex (and, in different ways, our simplest) feelings are betrayed by the words we use to try to express them. I think maybe I didn't express myself well enough, and that the topic is worth revisiting. I would like to revise and extend my remarks. One of the epigraphs from Stendhal's *The Red and the Black*, which is credited to R. P. Malagrida, goes like this: "Speech has been given to man to conceal his thought." Plenty of people have agreed with Stendhal. Mark Stewart, of the Bristol postpunkers Pop Group, concurred a century and a half later in "Words Disobey Me" (1979).

> *Truth is a feeling*
> *But it's not a sound*
> *We don't need words*
> *Throw them away*

The point's made again in "In Other Words" (1982), a surprisingly guitar-heavy Sly and the Family Stone demo.

> *When I hear you talking and I feel what you say*
> *It sounds a little funny cause the words are in the way*
> *I get the meaning that the words can't steal*
> *In other words, I hear what you feel*

And it's (re)made (yet) again in "Language Is a Virus" (1986), a funny little Laurie Anderson number in which a friend suspects her of performing her speech rather than feeling it. (The title and chorus are taken from a William S. Burroughs quote, "Language is a virus from outer space"; he's her Malagrida.)

> *Well I was talking to a friend*
> *And I was saying*

I wanted you
And I was looking for you
But I couldn't find you
I couldn't find you

This musing throws the friend off balance, as you might expect. Why would she be worrying about his absence in his presence? It seems a little . . . self-absorbed? That's his feeling, too.

And he said: Hey!
Are you talking to me?
Or are you just practicing
For one of those performances of yours? Huh?

Some may hold that the limits of language are the limits of the world, but others insist that language must be set aside before you can feel your way down to the truth. That argument is advanced, and then immediately undermined, by the great Smokey Robinson. He makes his case on "When the Words from Your Heart Get Caught Up in Your Throat," a B-side from 1968. The lyrics are tremendous throughout, but best when Robinson layers his metaphors—perfectly.

I have so much confidence when I'm by myself
It's like my nerves wore an armored coat
But baby now you're such a charmer you melt that coat
    of armor
And the words from my heart get caught up in my throat

The music lets the lyrics down somewhat, which can happen with late Miracles songs. And while a hyperarticulate song about being tongue-tied may be a peculiar kind of grandstand play, that's the genius of Smokey Robinson. In the last verse, he says that he prepared for his date by reading "some sweet poetry [he] could quote": He might be talking about Shakespeare, about Beatrice's lament in *Much Ado About Nothing* that "men are only turned into tongue"; or the way Iago, in *Othello*, describes Emilia's reticence by saying that "she puts her tongue a little in her heart"; or how the Clown, in *Twelfth Night*, explains that "words are very rascals since bonds disgraced them." But it's just as likely that he's talking about his own lyrics—that he's not reading Shakespeare, in other words, because he's writing something just as good.

If the song recognizes that clear communication is an illusion, it also implies that it is only one of many. You may not be able to say what you mean or mean what you say, but you also can't believe what you see or feel, as he explains in "The Love I Saw in You Was Just a Mirage." It's a justly famous song—it went top twenty and appears on all the anthologies—that remains the most devastating account of romantic illusion in pop music history. It has a somewhat concise story: Boy meets girl, boy loves girl, girl pretends to love boy, boy wakes up one day to discover that his heart has been ripped out of his chest by girl's deceitful ways. It's been around as long as there have been boys, girls, and hearts. But the lyric is peerless. Robinson talks about a romance that's gone bad, to the point where he questions to what degree it was good. People like to mention the famous Bob Dylan quote in which he referred to Smokey Robinson as "America's greatest living poet." I just wish it was clear how unironic a statement it was.

> *Just a minute ago your love was here*
> *All of a sudden it seemed to disappear*
> *The way you wrecked my life was like sabotage*
> *The love I saw in you was just a mirage*

The idea of a mirage may have been a little bit abstract for a pop song, so Smokey offered a compact two-line definition that is one of the best lines of poetry in the song. When it's sung, it's even better.

Just like the desert shows a thirsty man
A green oasis where there's only sand

This song, of course, gives the lie to the other one, which also gives the lie to itself, and as a result it's an instrument of tremendous hope beneath its message of hopelessness. This is exactly what language can do when it's not concealing or misrepresenting the truth—it can tell the truth in so many words.

Time moved on. Age came to Smokey, as it comes to everyone. Plastic surgery came to Smokey, perhaps more than it comes to everyone—sometimes it looks like he underwent some extra procedures that were earmarked for others. In 2004, he released a gospel album, *Food for the Spirit*, that was also a tie-in with Smokey Robinson Foods (slogan: "The Soul Is in the Bowl").

In 2006, he released an album of standards, *Timeless Love*, that was, in its own way, just as divided between art and commerce. Rod Stewart had just gone quintillion platinum or whatever with his American Songbook series, and others like Carly Simon had followed, so Smokey probably felt that it made sense to redeploy those songs with one of America's iconic voices.

The album was recorded with a small jazz combo, and the strings were added later to give the project more sonic foliage. Smokey's wavery tenor was still a thing of great beauty. And there was a clear, strong genealogy that linked the standards of the forties and fifties to the standards he had written in the sixties. "Fly Me to the Moon" had already been remade as a soul song by Bobby Womack, but Smokey's version went back to the beginning, to 1954, when the song was written by Bart Howard and recorded by Kaye Ballard. It was originally called

"In Other Words," and that was the meaning in addition to being the title. "Fly Me to the Moon" (the title was changed when Johnny Mathis recorded it in 1956) reiterates that true feelings don't require flowery language, that sometimes words get in the way of a simple message, but it also locates the consolation prize. If words didn't disobey us, if the words in our hearts didn't get caught up in our throats, if we had no fear, we might also have no poetry.

16

UP/DOWN

JUST LIKE A TEETER-TOTTER
Bar-Kays — *Animal*
Mercury/PolyGram: 1989

HAVE YOU EVER FELT YOURSELF SWITCHING PLACES WITH SOMEONE ELSE? It happens often in movies. Sometimes people even switch bodies with their moms. A few months ago I was talking to mine. She was in a dither. Is that a sexist term, a *dither*? I don't think so. Mr. Dithers was in *Blondie*, and he was a man, if not exactly a man's man. But my mother felt up in the air. She was thwarted by something, confused about what to do. She had found a woman's wallet on the street and mailed it back to her. The woman had sent my mother a reward of twenty dollars. My mother, feeling that the woman was young and relatively poor, thought that she should send the money back. My father had disagreed with the decision. "Keep it," he said. "She wants you to have it." She asked my opinion. "I'm six of one, half a dozen of the other," she said. "I'm right on the fence." She said that she needed to make a decision but didn't know what to do. I had no insight into the matter. I apologized for not being helpful. "That's okay," she said. "I've been unsure before."

A few days later, we switched places. I had a crisis at work. A cloud of uncertainty hung over my head. "Hi," my mother said. She was calling me on the phone. "How are things?" I told her. I sketched out my dilemma. "Oh," she said. She was on to other matters. She had no counsel. The situation displeased me—not the fact that I couldn't make up our mind, exactly, but the fact that we were out of sync. She was up, I was down. I was up, she was down. I spun the dial and landed back in 1989, with the Bar-Kays.

The Bar-Kays, of course, were a Memphis soul band that recorded the immortal "Soul Finger" in 1967, weathered a major tragedy when three members died in the plane crash that also claimed the life of Otis Redding, released a number of solid singles in the early seventies, and survived to become industry veterans despite steadily diminishing artistic returns. In 1989, they put out an album called *Animal*. If you haven't heard of it, then you belong to the vast majority of humanity. The best song on the album is the only good song on the album, and it hardly sounds like the Bar-Kays at all. That song, "Just Like a Teeter-Totter," was created in collaboration with Sly Stone, and from the first, it sets out to destabilize.

> *It's just as easy to see as it is to say*
> *It looks like it's free, but you will have to pay*

And then, later, he moves from the financial to the religious.

> *You remember the prayer, but you forgot how to pray*
> *When you learn how to swear, you got less to say*
> *It can't be wrong when it's right*
> *When you lie in the day, you lie awake at night*

The writing is typical of Sly's work during that period, deceptively simple and ultimately maddening. As the title suggests, the song is broadly concerned with not being able to make up your mind, and the music falls in line behind the lyrics. "Just Like a Teeter-Totter" shudders and judders. It lurches through time, both thwarting and enabling perspective (the "see" and "saw" that keep surfacing are not just two halves of the same word, but also the same verb in different tenses). The arrangement is bare-bones in the most frightening sense; it feels like a rib cage that has yet to be covered by flesh, or has recently been uncovered. The chorus is where the Bar-Kays meet Bartleby, and the song not only dramatizes the problem of equivocation but also locates the solution in annihilating all choice.

Just like a teeter-totter
Don't know if you oughta

A few days after my mom and I were out of sync, I called her. I had resolved my problem and she had dealt with hers, too. "I sent the money back," she said. I asked her if she knew the Bar-Kays song. "Nope," she said. "Send it to me."

I said I would. I didn't.

17

LIES/TRUTH

LA LA LA LIES
The Who — *The Who Sings My Generation*
MCA: 1965

IT'S NOT TRUE
The Who — *The Who Sings My Generation*
MCA: 1965

DON'T YOU LIE TO ME
Chuck Berry — *New Juke Box Hits*
Chess: 1961

LOVE IS THE LIE THAT YOU BELIEVE
Boyce Day — *Love Is the Lie That You Believe*
Black Fly: 2004

WHITE LIES
Nils Lofgren and Grin — *1+1*
Spindizzy: 1972

LITTLE GIRL LIES
Blondie — *Blondie*
Private Stock: 1976

EVERYBODY IS A FUCKING LIAR
The Posies
Demo recorded 1995
Available on: *At Least, At Last*
Not Lame: 2000

THE LIAR
Rev. Isaiah Shelton
Released 1927
Available on: *Goodbye, Babylon*
Dust-to-Digital: 2003

A GUY I WORK WITH BROUGHT A PLATE OF COOKIES THAT HIS WIFE HAD baked. He set them on a table. Another woman came by, picked one up, and took a bite out of it. They were raisin, not chocolate chip, and she was done with them. She put the bitten cookie back. The guy returned. "Hey," he said. "Who took a bite of this cookie?"

"Ben did," the woman said. "I saw him."

I leapt up from my desk. "No," I said. "You did!"

"Don't get so angry," she said. "It's nothing to worry about. It's just a cookie. He doesn't care if you took a bite out of it."

"I don't," the man said.

"Fine," I said. "But I didn't. She did." I pointed at her. I raised my voice above appropriate office volume. I slammed a stapler down hard. I was not in my right mind. But I was right.

My inability to handle a tiny lie may seem paradoxical, or even hypocritical. I'm a fiction writer. But like most fiction writers, I will insist that every event in every story in every book I have published is true. Just because they didn't happen doesn't mean they're lies. Sometimes the truth is even greater than in nonfiction, because fiction frees us up to talk about things we couldn't address directly. We can confess our feelings for others, our fears about moving through the world, our insecurities and superstitions.

Rock music has a similarly low tolerance for lying. At some level, of course, rock music is built on a foundational lie: white British kids pretending to be black American bluesmen and R&B shouters. But that's imposture rather than deception. Truth—or at the very least, the appearance of truth—is at the center of rock music. Authenticity matters. This is partly because many rock songs are about love and about ego, and those are the two substances most likely to combust when a lie is introduced. Take the Who's "La La La Lies" (1965), from their debut album *The Who Sings My Generation*. Like most early Who, there's a tension in the song between the boyish, almost tame vocals (not to mention Nicky Hopkins's jaunty piano) and the epochal drums and guitar—the eruption after the second chorus, courtesy of Keith Moon's drums and Pete Townshend's guitar, pushes the song rudely past mere pop. The narrator in the song is insisting that his girlfriend wasn't able to draw blood with her dishonesty, at least not in the way that she wanted. The lies under consideration here are pretty vague, which probably means he knows exactly what they are.

> *Don't ever think you made me mad*
> *I didn't listen to your lies*

A few songs later on the album, "It's Not True" (1965) sharpens the focus; here there are specific rumors that need to be debunked.

> *I haven't got eleven kids*
> *I weren't born in Baghdad*
> *I'm not half-Chinese either*
> *And I didn't kill my dad*

The Who wasn't the only foundational rock act to demonstrate a preoccupation with dishonesty. Chuck Berry, four years earlier, had reworked Tampa Red's 1940 blues number "Don't You Lie to Me" (1961), speeding up the tempo and using a tricky shuffle beat (I think it's Fred Below drumming) but keeping many of the lyrics.

> *There's two kinds of people that I just can't stand*
> *Well, that's a lying woman and a cheating man*

Berry says he gets "shook up as a man can be," which is unpleasant, and not just for the person who's being lied to: A verse later, Berry explains that the lies make him "evil as a man can be." The Rolling Stones took a crack at the song in 1964, and they reordered the choruses, getting evil before they got all shook up. They also changed the title by taking out the *You*. It's all a question of where the lie's effect eventually lands.

If you start collecting songs about lying and liars, you'll find that there are a million, and that all of them are good. Okay, maybe that's an exaggeration, but it's not a lie. Big Star's "Don't Lie to Me" (1972), which isn't the same song as the Tampa Red / Berry composition, is the hardest-rocking three minutes the band ever put on record. Jackie Wilson's "Stop Lying" (1966) preaches cold, hard emotional truth underneath a cotton-candy arrangement of horns, chimes, and backup vocals. There are songs about the romantic benefits of untruth, like Fleetwood Mac's aerodynamic "Little Lies" (1987). There are songs about its drawbacks, like Asha Puthli's erotically vengeful "Lies" (1973). There are songs with deception woven into the plot, like Pedro the Lion's "Bad Diary Days" (1998). There are broader political settings, like John Lennon's "Gimme Some Truth" (1971). There are manifestos, like the Castaways' "Liar Liar" (1965) and the Sex Pistols' "Liar" (1977). If anyone ever lies to you, you're not going to have to look far for a playlist.

Some of the best songs are the subtler ones. Boyce Day's "Love Is the Lie That You Believe" (2004) catalogs various types of deception, and concludes that self-deception is sometimes the only thing that can start the engine of the heart.

> *You can tell me all about Santa Claus*
> *The Fountain of Youth and the Wizard of Oz*
> *I don't believe God took the form of a dove*
> *So how come I believe in love?*

Self-deception of a different sort is the prime mover in "White Lies" (1972). Grin was the band led by Nils Lofgren, who was a teen-age veteran of Neil Young's band and went on to play guitar for the E Street Band. "White Lies" was a cult hit that had all the markings of a massive hit—angelic harmonies, a punch-it-out chorus, and a thrilling false ending. Maybe what held it back was its message, which is tricky. Lofgren seems to be warning a woman not to spread the rumor that he loves her, but he seems to be lying mostly to himself.

> *Think I may be daydreamin', baby, but I know*
> *I know what I still don't mean to you*
> *While I try, don't start tellin'*
> *White lies, you better talk it over*
> *Everywhere I go I'm hearin' white lies*
> *Tellin' everybody that I love you*

And Blondie's "Little Girl Lies" (1976) is a girl-group update that puts straightforward carnality where euphemism used to be.

> *He loves her so much, he don't wanna lose her*
> *And there's no other girl he likes to ball better*
> *But he's busy tonight, "We'll make it tomorrow"*
> *He's telling his little girl lies*

Most of these songs are about lying in love. That may be at the root of the Posies' "Everybody Is a Fucking Liar" (1995), but the band widens the scope considerably. In the end, the tack taken is theological, almost.

> *Just as God in his infinite infancy thinks he's in control*
> *That's when God in his infinite infamy decides to damn*
>   *our souls*
> *Let's throw it all in and think of places to back up and*
>   *begin*
> *To build something higher*
> *'Cause everybody is a fucking liar*

The Rev. Isaiah Shelton believes in a somewhat different relationship between truth and God. "The Liar" (1927) is a driving R&B number beneath the gospel—it provided the melody for Ray Charles's "Leave My Woman Alone" (1956)—but when you're talking about something as serious as lying, it's better to end on a comic note. I once dated a woman who insisted that the funniest lyric in pop music came in Nine Inch Nails' "Terrible Lie" (1989), when Trent Reznor, after lamenting the meaninglessness of existence, raged to the Lord above, "Hey God, I think you owe me a great big apology." She had a mental picture of Reznor standing beneath a stormy sky, shaking his fist furiously, as if God had wrongfully accused him of taking a bite out of a cookie. "A great big apology!" she said. "Can you even believe it?" She started laughing every time she thought about it. I don't exactly remember why we broke up, but I know it wasn't because of a lie, and that's why I remember her fondly.

TEXT/VOICE

VOICES
Cheap Trick — *Dream Police*
Epic: 1979

YOUR SWEET VOICE
Matthew Sweet — *Girlfriend*
Zoo Entertainment / BMG: 1991

I HEARD THE VOICE OF A PORKCHOP
Jim Jackson
Released 1928
Available on: *Good for What Ails You: Music of the Medicine Shows, 1926–1937*
Old Hat: 2006

THE THING THAT WE CALL A TELEPHONE IS, THESE DAYS, ACTUALLY A nodal point for several other kinds of communication that have little or nothing to do with telephony, from texting to e-mailing. This evolution has had several major effects, but the main one is this: There are days when I talk to friends but I don't hear their voices. In a literary sense, this isn't quite true: I read things that they write, so I learn their voices, but the physical fact of their voices is less real than ever: air, cords, tongue. A few years ago, I got back in touch with a friend after a long hiatus. Since high school, in fact. We reconnected on e-mail. Soon after we started talking (writing) again, she was talking (writing) about someone's voice in her office. The idea struck me as strange. I could imagine that person's voice, since she was describing it, but I had no information about *her* voice. Had it changed over time? Was it roughened up by whiskey? Deepened by age? Stealthy? Persuasive? Careful? Candied? I didn't ask, because that would have been embarrassing, but I wondered, and wondered if anyone ever asks. What does your voice sound like? It's an intimate question, and intimacy means different things than it used to.

Though the world has less speech, it also has more chatter, and pop music is one of the sites of that paradox. You can't listen to pop for more than a minute or two without thinking about voices: why this one is better than that one, why that one is more affecting than the other one, why a certain technical ability fails to convey a certain kind of honesty. Magazines are constantly running features about the best voices in the history of the genre. Is Dylan better than Sam Cooke? Is Christina Aguilera better than Grace Slick? Is Ian Hunter better than Stephen Malkmus? Is Bobbie Gentry better than Beyoncé? Every answer to these questions is right, and every answer is wrong, but the questions themselves are the point: It is the voices that are being considered.

And yet, even within a genre universally defined by voices, there are only a few songs that are specifically about voices. Cheap Trick's "Voices" (1979) is one, and one of the best, because the melody is sweet without being saccharine, and because Robin Zander has a better voice than most singers. It's not about a conversation, but about the memory of a conversation, and about how memory can polish a lover's voice.

> *I remember every word you said*
> *I remember voices in my head*

One of the secret truths about voices is revealed here, which is that they are mostly for other people. Singers probably know this instinctively, but it's nice when they write songs that sharpen and drive home the point. When other people give you their voice, even a few moments of it, you can yoke it to your own emotions, use it for your own purposes. Their voice, moving through the air, enables your inner voice. This idea is handled even more explicitly, and even more self-referentially, in Matthew Sweet's "Your Sweet Voice" (1991).

> *Speak to me with your sweet voice*
> *And take me through another night*

Speak to me with your sweet voice
And I will surely be all right

Try to read this with the name pun stripped away. Or rather, try to hear it with the pun silenced. I can't. It sounds like he's at once pleading with a woman and marketing his own work. I once spent the night with a woman whose voice I really liked. I like the voices of everyone I've ever been involved with (how can you not? a bad voice would be intolerable), but this one woman had a tremendous voice. I told her so, that night, all the time, until I realized that when I was telling her things, she wasn't talking.

Since I started writing this piece, my phone has chimed twice. That's two more voice mails I'll be listening to, two more voices that will, no matter the information being relayed, leave me slightly cold.

I remember when my younger son was four, when he had just recently started reading. It was also the time when he had started to learn the process by which language becomes immortal (or is it tragically attenuated?) in the printed word. Up until then, as a preliterate but already verbal child, he had only one option for expressing himself—talking, which he did constantly. He talked and talked, and if using your voice was a form of generosity, he was the most charitable being I know.

Sometimes, when words filled up his head, he pretended that inanimate things were speaking to him: fire hydrants, cars, stuffed animals. I remember one night in particular from when he was five. He was supposed to read my wife a book after she read him a book. Instead, he picked up a stuffed dog and let it do the reading for him. The dog read well. It was funny, because he made no real attempt to differentiate the dog's voice from his own, and it was also something other than funny, because it illustrated how firmly he was located inside a world of voices. That has since changed. He is older now. He has no illusions about stuffed dogs speaking to him, or to anyone else, for that matter.

You could make the argument that one of the dividing lines between childhood and adulthood is the moment when we stop pretending that inanimate things are talking to us, but then you'd have to contend with the counterargument, brilliantly expressed in Jim Jackson's "I Heard the Voice of a Porkchop," from 1928.

> *I heard the voice of a porkchop say, "Come unto me and rest"*
> *Well, you talk about your stewing meats: I ain't know what's the best*
> *You talk about your chicken, ham, and eggs, and turkey stuffed in dress*
> *But I heard the voice of a porkchop say, "Come unto me and rest"*

Here, the porkchop is talking in the voice of the Savior. Jackson is lampooning Matthew 11:28 (no relation to Matthew Sweet) and the popular hymn based on it, but he's transplanting the divine comfort to something much more earthy. Puzzle out the song on your own time, slowly, and give me a call when it's unpuzzled. I'll pick up.

19

SECRETS/REVELATIONS

CAN U KEEP A SECRET
De La Soul — *3 Feet High and Rising*
Tommy Boy: 1989

I HAVE A SECRET
Half Japanese — *Sing No Evil*
Iridescence: 1985

SECRET LOVE
Billy Stewart
Released 1967
Available on: *20th Century Masters—The Millennium Collection: The Best of Billy Stewart*
MCA: 2000

YOUR SECRET'S SAFE WITH ME
The Robert Cray Band — *Don't Be Afraid of the Dark*
Mercury: 1988

THE SECRET
Slapp Happy
Recorded 1973
Available on: *Acnalbasac Noom*
Recommended: 1980

MY DIRTY SECRET IS A DIVINE DILEMMA
Banner Barbados
Demo recorded 2005

HERE IS A MOMENT FROM THE EARLY NINETIES I WOULD LIKE TO FREEZE in time. I was dating a woman in another city a thousand miles west of Brooklyn. We woke up one morning, got dressed, and went to get coffee. She had her head down in her mug and was breathing in the coffee steam with more determination than usual. Then she raised her gaze to meet mine. "I have to tell you something," she said.

I knew immediately that she was about to tell me a secret. I had a number of thoughts, all at once. First, I was excited. It seemed like a step forward in our relationship. Then I was curious whether I could guess her secret in the few seconds before she revealed it to me. I think I preferred that I be able to do so, both to soften the blow and to prevent our relationship from being exposed as the kind of relationship that needed a boost in intimacy. I foresuffered a feeling of anticlimax. She would tell me whatever it was and I would receive it and process it, and then what? We'd finish our coffee? We'd go back home? I'd worry about what other secrets lay beneath the surface? A black curtain would fall down over the world?

She told me the secret. I won't say what it was. It belonged to the class of things that young people early in a relationship believe they should tell their partners. Maybe it was that she had slept with someone else. Maybe it was that her father was an alcoholic. Maybe it was that she had a strange habit of taking the hair that collected in the shower drain and putting it into her mouth. Maybe it was that she once mastur-bated on a train. Maybe it was that she stole money from a roommate at camp and blamed the theft on another girl. Like I said, I won't say. What I will say is my reaction to her secret exactly echoed the thoughts I had had just before she revealed it. I was excited, then I was comforted that my internal guess had been roughly accurate, then I was disappointed. She had told me something about herself that wasn't exactly interesting, except in the sense that I hadn't known it a minute earlier. Now what?

There are other kinds of secrets, obviously. There are secrets you can tell about others without their consent. In the late eighties and early nineties, there was a boomlet of stories outing gay celebrities. I was just out of college then, and at least a few friends (whether straight, gay, or hanging in the balance) had strong opinions about the propriety of exposing someone else's innermost secrets. The year that Michelangelo Signorile founded *Out* magazine, De La Soul released *3 Feet High and Rising*. One of my friends, who was struggling to come out to his parents, thought that "Can U Keep a Secret" (1989) was staging a trivial version of the outing process.

> *Mase has big fat dandruff*
> *Trugoy has dandruff*
> *Everybody in the world, you have dandruff*

The most common secret in pop music is somewhere in the middle—it's secret love. There's Ron Sexsmith's "Secret Heart" (1995), the Miracles' "I Love You Secretly" (1973), and Half Japanese's "I Have a Secret" (1985), in which Jad Fair yowls out his heart's deepest desires.

> *Someone sent you roses, Karen*
> *Oh, isn't that nice, Karen*
> *Yeah that's twice this week, isn't it, Karen?*
> *You're a lucky girl, Karen*

We can all agree that this is a noble and even majestic secret: Just listen to Billy Stewart's "Secret Love" (1967), a remake of an earlier Doris Day hit, and it's just as exuberant and idiosyncratic as Stewart's cover of George and Ira Gershwin's "Summertime" (1966).

The kind of secret under consideration here, the kind that can emerge with a frisson early in a relationship, however, is different. Think of something minor, shameful, purely personal. At the beginning of the piece, when I listed the possible secrets revealed by my girlfriend in another city, I included chewing on hair from the shower drain grate. Those are the kinds of secrets I mean—bad habits and fetishes, the revelation of which might temporarily make a new lover feel closer. Think of them as dandruff on the inside. What reason is there to share those things? None, I think. They should not be served up. No one wants to eat that dish.

Sometimes secrets are presented, and sometimes they are extracted. Here's a secret: The half story I told at the beginning of the piece, about my unidentifiable girlfriend in a city west of here, isn't exactly true. Everything in my description—the way she lowered her face into the coffee steam, the way she raised her head to meet my gaze—happened, but something else happened before that. I pushed half a muffin across my plate, sighed heavily, and said, "Tell me a secret."

I blame sex and high spirits, and the fear that I wouldn't have them for much longer. I thought I might lose this woman if I didn't seal the seams of our very new relationship. So I asked her for a secret.

Six months later, we weren't dating anymore. The secret she told me didn't ruin us, but the impulse to ask for it may have. Asking for a secret in such a flagrant manner appears to be a gesture of intimacy, when in fact it is nothing of the sort. A secret that is requested or presented plainly is a form of currency and too often a bond that hasn't matured.

When you have a secret, what do you do with it? You either tell it all over town or you keep it safe, like a seed inside of your heart. But dark seeds flower into dark blossoms. In the Robert Cray Band's "Your Secret's Safe with Me" (1988), a man who has been coveting a woman across the way watches in horror as she betrays her boyfriend with a new lover. Though the production is slicker than on Cray's breakthrough album, *Strong Persuader*, the song advances a powerful brand of the Memphis soul that has increasingly become his calling card.

> *Baby, you should keep your bedroom shades pulled down*
> *I can see right in, I've seen you in that black nightgown*
> *I've seen you with your lover when your man is out of town*
> *But don't worry, babe, your secret's safe with me*

Instances of shared secrets actually leading to happiness are rare and often precious. Slapp Happy's "The Secret" (1973), a Peter Blegvad–Anthony Moore composition sung by Dagmar Krause, is a strange little gem of a pop song that describes the rare case of intimacy that's forged by holding on to something for someone else.

> *He's making my days into night*
> *Mercury man does everything he can*
> *And my only plan is to keep his secret secret*

Banner Barbados, a band from Seattle that made a splash online with a Velvet Underground–ish song called "Since You Caught My Eye," had a second standout single that sped through a Stones-y riff into jangly, organ-driven mayhem that conflated theological and romantic revelation. The band disappeared without a trace, as far as I know, but their song is an appropriate place to conclude, because it gives away the real secret: that God is in the details.

About a year ago, a friend of mine was dating two men. One of them screwed his courage up and, over drinks, asked her for a secret. I think she complied with the hair-chewing thing. The other one never raised the issue of secrets. He put in his time, made lots of small talk, noticed things about her, and eventually knew her well enough that the secrets were superfluous. The goal is not to deliver or receive secrets on demand, but to get them as part of a steady flow, to know another person rather than another person's secrets.

QUESTIONS/ANSWERS

WHO LOVES THE SUN
The Velvet Underground – *Loaded*
Cotillion/Atlantic: 1970

WHO WAS THAT MASKED MAN
Van Morrison – *Veedon Fleece*
Warner Bros.: 1974

WHO WOULD YOU FUCK
Ghostface Killah – *Supreme Clientele*
Razor Sharp / Epic: 2000

WHO TOOK THE MERRY OUT OF CHRISTMAS
The Staple Singers
Released 1970
Available on: *The Complete Stax / Volt Soul Singles, Vol. 2: 1968–1971*
Stax: 1993

WHO SLAPPED JOHN
Gene Vincent
Released 1956
Available on: *The Road Is Rocky: The Complete Studio Masters, 1956–1971*
Bear Family: 2005

WHO SHOT SAM
George Jones
Released 1959
Available on: *Cup of Loneliness: The Classic Mercury Years*
Mercury/PolyGram: 1994

WHO DONE IT?
Harry Nilsson – *Knnillssonn*
RCA Victor: 1977

WHO THREW THE WHISKEY IN THE WELL
Wynonie Harris
Released 1945 (as by Lucky Millinder and His Orchestra)
Available on: *Big Band, Blues & Boogie: Roots of Rock 'n' Roll, Vol. 1*
President: 2003

I KNOW WHO THREW THE WHISKEY (IN THE WELL)
Bull Moose Jackson
Released 1945
Available on: *Greatest Hits: My Big Ten Inch*
King: 1996

I HAD GUESTS OVER AT MY HOUSE THIS WEEK, INCLUDING SOME I DIDN'T know very well, and I had to decide where to set my level of curiosity. Pitch it too low and people feel neglected. Pitch it too high and they feel scrutinized. I think I worked it out, but it's a struggle for me and always has been—not because I find it hard to ask questions, but I find it hard to stop once I've started. It's always been that way. As a kid, I dressed up as Sherlock Holmes for Halloween, and that authorized me to look at things closely, squint, and then ask a number of inappropriate questions. (Some years, when the nearby adults got lazy or my dad didn't have a spare pipe, I was a cat burglar, and I imagined that I was committing crimes that Sherlock Holmes would have to solve the following year.)

For these reasons, I've always been drawn to question songs. There are all kinds of inquiries, from "Where did our love go?" to "When will I be loved?" but I prefer who songs. Not Who songs, though those are frequently great, but "who" songs: Who made who? Who do you love? Who says a funk band can't play rock? Some of these who songs are the jumping-off point for broader inquiries. The Velvet Underground's "Who Loves the Sun" (1970), which is a kind of pessimistic response to the Beatles' "Here Comes the Sun" (1969), features what might be

Doug Yule's best lead vocal, which isn't saying much. But "Who Was That Masked Man" (1974) features what might be Van Morrison's best lead vocal, which *is* saying much.

> *Oh, ain't it lonely*
> *When you're livin' with a gun*
> *Well, you can't slow down and you can't turn 'round*
> *And you can't trust anyone*

The title comes from the Lone Ranger and possibly Lenny Bruce, but the song comes from somewhere far stranger. It's on *Veedon Fleece*, Morrison's strangest and most elemental album, which was written and recorded (quickly) after his divorce from Janet Planet. Throughout the record, Morrison uses a mournful falsetto, which is a vocal approach that he didn't employ often in his earliest records and almost certainly can't employ anymore. It's eerily effective in "Who Was That Masked Man," where Morrison weighs the value of stardom against the value of private identity and comes down right in the middle.

> *When the ghost comes 'round at midnight*
> *Well, you both can have some fun*
> *He can drive you mad, he can make you sad*
> *He can keep you from the sun*

Question songs don't have to be ontological. Some are specific challenges, like Bill Withers's "Who Is He (And What Is He to You)?" (1972), in which romantic doubt becomes jealous certainty. (The song, complete with its unforgettable four-note clusters—four up, four down—was later gender-reupholstered by Me'Shell Ndegéocello.) Some are games, like the overlong Ghostface skit that rates potential bedmates (Lil' Kim or Foxy Brown? Lady of Rage or Rah Digga? Janet or Chrissy?). And still others are polemics: the Staple Singers' "Who

Took the Merry Out of Christmas" (1970), which is a kind of unholy holy cross between Marvin Gaye's "Inner City Blues (Make Me Wanna Holler)" (1971) and the gospel standard "Be with Me Jesus."

Then there are the songs that pose true mysteries. The first one takes us all the way back to 1956. Gene Vincent was already well along the road to rockabilly immortality, thanks in no small part to the guitar of Cliff Gallup, when he recorded "Who Slapped John." In the song, there's a party. There's a question of relations. And then there's a crime, sort of.

> *Well, John jumped up, then he screamed*
> *"Well, she's my gal, man, and that I mean"*
> *Well, who-who, who slapped John?*
> *Who-who, who slapped John?*
> *Baby, who slapped John when the lights went low-oh?*

Three years after the lights went low-oh, George Jones cowrote and recorded "Who Shot Sam" (1959). It's an echo of and possibly even an answer record to "Who Slapped John," but it's also linked to the folk tradition of complex story-songs that would later reach its apogee/nadir with Bob Dylan's "Lily, Rosemary, and the Jack of Hearts" (1975). The Jones song counts among its characters Sammy Samson, Silly Mill, Flirty Mirty, the police chief, the judge, and the narrator. There's also a lyric that might be cryptically filthy.

> *We met Silly Milly, everything was all right*
> *Her eyes started rollin', we shoulda went a-bowlin'*
> *Wham-bam, who shot Sam, my-my*

"Who Shot Sam" is mentioned in the opening line of Elvis Costello's "Motel Matches," and within two years Costello would be covering and performing with Jones.

"Who Slapped John" and "Who Shot Sam" remain unsolved. And in the end, they're minor crimes, mere party (or roadhouse) mayhem. Neither has the production values or the narrative drive of Harry Nilsson's "Who Done It?" (1977). Nilsson had already recorded a murder mystery, of sorts, with "Ten Little Indians" (1967); "Who Done It?" revives the calypso stylings of "Coconut" (1972) for a closed-door manor-house murder mystery that's straight out of Agatha Christie. The song is from the underrated album *Knnillssonn*, whose double-exposure cover image doubles its doubled typography, and it's pushed along by a lovely, confusing string part that sounds like a sample in a hip-hop song. Nilsson's vocals are not as angelic as they once were; he ruptured his vocal cords while making *Pussy Cats* with John Lennon. But it's a committed performance, if you mean commitment to irony. There are Smythes, Sloans, Chopin quotations (the Piano Sonata No. 2), and a superb alibi from Nilsson's narrator ("I was in Colorado, having breakfast, with a nun!"). In the end, like much of Nilsson's best work, it's a very high-level novelty record, and all the more personal for its impersonality.

We should close with the saddest mystery of all. "Who Threw the Whiskey in the Well" (1945) is credited to Wynonie Harris, though in fact the song was originally released by Lucky Millinder and His Orchestra, with Harris as a vocalist. The song became a hit, and Harris, who was not under contract, went off to seek his fortune as a solo artist. In addition to kicking off that solo career (which yielded such hits as "Mr. Blues Jumped the Rabbit" [ca. 1947], "Bloodshot Eyes" [1954], and "Good Rockin' Tonight" [1954]), the song produced an answer record by Bull Moose Jackson, who had replaced Harris in Millinder's orchestra. So who did throw the whiskey in the well? Find out yourself. No need to spoil the ending.

ATTENTION/INATTENTION

CRYING FOR ATTENTION
Graham Parker — *Another Grey Area*
Arista: 1982

IGNORE ME
The Gas — 7-inch single
Polydor: 1981

LOVE AIN'T NO TOY
Yvonne Fair — *The Bitch Is Black*
Motown: 1975

WHAT AM I WORTH
Dave Alvin — *King of California*
Hightone: 1994

OVER THE HOLIDAYS I WAS WATCHING A SHOW ON CABLE AND NOTICED that a character had the same name as a woman I used to know, and not just the same name but the same exact name: first, middle, last. The show was terrible, something about a diner and a baby and an escaped convict, but it got me thinking about the woman, and the talks we used to have, and specifically one of the last talks we had, in which she told me that I didn't pay her enough attention.

I remembered that final conversation first. It was the only thing I could recall clearly. It was in May, though the weather was summer weather. We were sitting in her apartment, which was just off the campus of the college she attended. Some friends of mine had been in town that night, and we had all gone to dinner. The wine she drank at dinner, and the glass or two she added back at the apartment, had made her expansive, and over the course of the evening she navigated through a virtuosic consideration of all the things she liked to discuss: clothes, sex, art, whether all duty was unconditional, Guns N' Roses, Aeschylus. She was at once profoundly brainy and prodigiously trivial, and if it wasn't a calculated philosophy, it should have been. Finally, just when I thought it was time for the wine to produce pantlessness, she pulled up short and told me that I had hurt her feelings during dinner. "You ignored me," she said. "I need you to pay attention to me more than you do."

I laughed it off. She was being ridiculous and I said so. I was paying attention to her at dinner and, more importantly, afterward, and if she couldn't see that, it was her fault. She said it was okay and that she wasn't upset and I, a fool, believed her. A few weeks after that, we weren't dating anymore—did I mention that we were dating?—and then a few months after that, we weren't friends anymore.

Her memory, or at least my memory of her, is inseparable from the music I played when I spent time with her. Graham Parker's "Crying for Attention" (1982) was one of the songs that was on heavy rotation. Like many Graham Parker songs, it has made itself known by degrees. At the time, it was just another decent track on a solid but unspectacular record—not *Squeezing Out Sparks*, not even *Stick to Me*. But every time the knottiness of unrequited love has tightened around me, I have come back to the song, and especially to the deceptive calm in the vocals and the midtempo arrangement.

> *Hey, sometimes everybody has to be the center of attraction*
> *But I never expect any satisfaction*
> *And I'm not crying, I'm not crying, I'm not crying*
> *Not crying for attention*

He's not crying for attention, except in the repeated lyrics about how he's not crying for attention. In my situation, it was a woman who wanted my attention, and who was brave enough to tell me so. In Parker's song, it's a man who wants the attention, and not just the sex he's getting (more than a handful). For me, the song turns on one line in particular: "I know my place—I just can't stay there." What's important is that the tendered offer isn't enough. Desire is by definition aspirational. If she had quoted that line to me, it might have done the trick. Instead, she was straightforward, and she suffered for it, and then I suffered.

What this brief autopsy excludes is an answer to the main question: Did I ignore her? Well, yes, probably. I had just come out of a relationship that meant more to me than she did, though this woman was more beautiful and more willing to risk herself emotionally than the other woman. I was still a little ashamed that things with the woman I loved more hadn't worked out. Even worse, I remember feeling like I was the one being ignored. I felt like she was unable to sense something essential about me. I didn't know "Ignore Me" by the Gas (1981) then, which is a shame, because it has an irresistible chorus that I could have shouted at her when we fought, which was often, as well as a perfectly inverted perspective that makes ignoring seem like an elevated form of paying attention. Instead, I told her the truth, which was that I didn't agree that there was a problem and that if there was I was sorry, because I simply didn't think I could do any better.

Nobody likes to hear this. Yvonne Fair was a singer with James Brown who became a solo star for a time in the seventies. Her most important solo recording, *The Bitch Is Black*, was a collaboration with Norman Whitfield and, from a distance of three decades, stands as one of the best funk diva albums of the time, far better than similar albums from Claudia Lennear or Marie "Queenie" Lyons. "Love Ain't No Toy" (1975) is one of the best of a set of consistently strong songs, and it plays like vintage Betty Davis, as reconceived by a woman who can actually sing.

> *I don't know what your friends call you*
> *When you're out in the street*
> *Romeo or Casanova*
> *To me you ain't nothing but a low-down cheat*

This is a song about cheating, not ignoring. Maybe Yvonne Fair thinks ignoring would have been better. I don't. I have said that the conversation about how I ignored her—the woman I was dating, not Yvonne Fair—was one of the last. That's somewhat misleading. We had addressed the issue of our failure many times, during the breakup and afterward. She would call me and say that she was thinking of me and that she couldn't understand exactly what went wrong. Had she been too needy? Had I been conflicted? I couldn't answer, not then. Even after a few years, after a few more tries with a few more women, I had no real idea.

There was no song that I knew that could explain our dilemma, not well. Then, years later, I bought Dave Alvin's *King of California*. Alvin was the songwriter behind the Blasters, a critically acclaimed band I never liked quite as much as I thought I should have. When he became a solo artist, his vocals waterlogged him further. But on *King of California*, which is filled with stripped-down, shuffling versions of old and new songs, he evolved from artlessness to a style that was wise, warm, and colloquial. The duet with Syd Straw on George Jones's "What Am I Worth" (1994) was, and is, my favorite. Both singers articulate the desire to be valued by the other, with the result being perfect romantic equipoise. But it's not just desire—it's desperation.

> *I don't know why you're making me cry*
> *Honey, won't you give me a clue*
> *What am I worth on God's great earth*
> *If I don't mean nothing to you*

That's how it should be—how it has to be. Attention is the currency of active relationships. It should be asked for, even demanded, without a second's uncertainty. If you don't feel good about asking for someone else's attention, then you're not standing in the right stream. People who say they have lots of space between them must mean only that they have translated hands-on (or eyes-on) attention to a different kind of attendance. If there's no real presence, then there's a real absence, which is why this woman and I broke up, and why I don't remember very much about her other than what I have related here. It doesn't feel good to remember someone so poorly.

LOCATION/DISLOCATION

THIS IS WHERE I BELONG
The Kinks
Recorded 1967
Available on: *The Kink Kronikles*
Reprise: 1972

THIS IS WHERE I BELONG
Bill Lloyd — *Set to Pop*
East Side Digital: 1994

THIS IS WHERE I BELONG
Frank Black — *Headache* (10-inch single)
4AD: 1994

THIS IS WHERE I BELONG
Ron Sexsmith
Available on: *This Is Where I Belong: The Songs of Ray Davies & The Kinks*
Rykodisc: 2002

YOU BELONG TO ME
Rev. Tom Frost — *South of Hell, France*
Closed for Private Party: 2006

IT'S HARD TO LIKE THE KINKS BECAUSE OF WES ANDERSON. NO. I SAID it wrong. What I mean is that now, as opposed to a decade ago, it's hard to make sense of exactly how much I like the glory period of the Kinks, in part because the cultural overtones of those early songs have become highly specific as a result of their inclusion in various Wes Anderson films. Everyone knows what I mean, right? This is just an introductory paragraph and I don't want it to get too clotted. Suffice it to say that "Nothin' in This World Can Stop Me Worryin' 'Bout That Girl" (1965) used to mean a tremendous amount to me, and now it means something to me about *Rushmore*. The same goes for "Powerman" (1970) and *The Darjeeling Limited*. I come neither to praise nor to bury the filmmaker. I just want to—need to—note that he and his production designers have interfered with an entire generation's pristine experience of a few Kinks songs. The same is probably true of Scorsese and the Stones, or Quentin Tarantino and certain artifacts of seventies soft rock. But it's probably most true of Wes Anderson and the Kinks.

It's a shame for many songs, but for some more than others. "This Is Where I Belong," one of Ray Davies's most perfectly realized compositions (and, incidentally, one that has not yet surfaced in a Wes Anderson movie), was originally released as the B-side of a Dutch single in April 1967, which is the rough equivalent of James Joyce originally publishing "Araby" in the back of a program for a boat show. The song's absurd obscurity was rectified when it was included on the 1972 compilation *The Kink Kronikles*, and it has also been on subsequent expanded versions of the great LP *Face to Face*. Today, it resides on your local streaming services. Easy to find, easy to hear. The song is sad, joyous, short, and eternal, as Davies explains everything he knows about devotion, which also happens to be everything everyone else will ever need to know. This is an exaggeration, but not by much.

> *I can't think of a place I'd rather be*
> *The whole wide world doesn't mean so much to me*
> *For this is where I belong*

Later, Davies addresses the prospect of wealth, and its relative insufficiency when compared to emotional location.

> *I won't search for a house upon a hill*
> *Why should I when I'd only miss you still*
> *For this is where I belong*

When a song is this eloquent, there's not much left to say. What I can say is that I was thinking of it most of the week, because I had two conversations with friends about relationships that seemed to be entering phases of difficulty. The situations are entirely different from one another, but one of the principal issues in each case was the feeling of belonging. The people who came to talk to me, one man and one woman, both questioned whether their partners could successfully keep them in the relationship, not sexually or financially but emotionally. One person said, "I wonder if she can locate me there," which seemed like a slightly incorrect use of the word *locate*, or at least a slightly stagy one, but I got the gist. The other person said, "I sometimes think I should be elsewhere, and that's wrong. I want to want to be there."

I have drifted a bit from the song, which is unfair. The brilliance of the lyric is everywhere, but it is most specifically located in the way that Davies conflates emotional and physical space. The "this" where he belongs moves through time, obviously. Love has to move through time or it is something else entirely: convenience or delusion. But it also moves through space, and when he says "I'd stay here anyway," he really means that he'll go anywhere so long as she goes. It's the song of a fellow traveler, not a nontraveler.

The song indeed enacts this principle. It travels well. In fact, one of the testaments to the greatness of "This Is Where I Belong" is that it is virtually indestructible when placed in the hands of a capable interpreter. Here I offer three examples: a lapidary little version by Bill Lloyd (though he changes the "I won't search" line, not for the better), a rough-and-tumble treatment by Frank Black (who also has problems searching for the house upon the hill; he gets a little too emotive after searching and disrupts the song's smooth surface), and a majestically mournful cover by Ron Sexsmith that rivals the original. "This Is Where I Belong" has close relatives: Bob Dylan's "She Belongs to Me" (1965), Rickie Lee Jones's "We Belong Together" (1981), Love's "Your Mind and We Belong Together" (1968), even the Dirtbombs' "Your Love Belongs Under a Rock" (2001). There is "You Belong to Me," the fifties standard that was made famous by Patti Page and Jo Stafford and then made less famous by the Rev. Tom Frost in 2006, and whose argument replaces Davies's expansive generosity with an equally expansive possessiveness.

There is much more to say about the difficulty (and importance) of belonging to another person. Limits must be set so that you do not vanish inside him or her. Dignity must be maintained so that you do not ask to belong to a club that will only have you as a member after a request has been made. Tactics must be employed to ensure that your mind roams without wandering. But these are gnomic precepts that don't advance the case much beyond where Ray Davies left it in 1967, in Holland, on a B-side.

ORIGINALITY/IMITATION

UNDER MY THUMB
The Rolling Stones — *Aftermath*
London: 1966

IT'S THE SAME OLD SONG
The Four Tops
Recorded 1965
Available on: *Anthology*
Motown: 1974

REVOLUTION
The Beatles
Released 1968
Available on: *Love*
Apple/Capitol: 2006

DO UNTO OTHERS
Pee Wee Crayton
Recorded 1954
Available on: *Pee Wee's Blues: The Complete Aladdin and Imperial Recordings*
Capitol: 1996

DA YA THINK I'M SEXY?
Rod Stewart — *Blondes Have More Fun*
Warner Bros.: 1978

(IF YOU WANT MY LOVE) PUT SOMETHING DOWN ON IT
Bobby Womack — *I Don't Know What the World Is Coming To*
United Artists: 1975

HOW MANY DAYS DO YOU SAY SOMETHING TRULY NEW? RECALCULATE after thinking about how many days you have asked yourself that question.

A friend texted me the other day. I was working, or pretending to work. These days, if you load the iMessage program onto your desktop, you can just text away, all the while pretending (or even telling yourself) that you are working. What did we used to do to pretend we were working? Daydream? All of that is gone.

"What should I do?" she asked. She was talking about a relationship. I had just been out to lunch, and a woman in the park had asked a friend the same question. The friend in the park had said, "Pretend like there's a case where you are happy, elsewhere, and that will help you see that this isn't the only option." It was sound enough counsel. When my friend texted me for advice, that was the advice I gave. I didn't think for five seconds. I just parroted back what I had recently heard. "Thanks," my friend said. "You always give such good advice."

I had mixed feelings about the compliment. On the one hand, it was a compliment, and I thrive on praise. On the other hand, I had lifted something and not suffered an ounce for it. That process, humiliating in some respects, comforting in others, got me thinking about originality and copying, which is one of the most fertile topics in pop music and indeed in all of culture. Are new ideas even possible? If you spin an old idea slightly, is it yours? If you copy and no one catches you, are you really free and clear, and what does it matter anyway? These are just some of the questions I stole from the bracing and provocative essay "Why Plagiarism Is Central to Creativity," by Robert Scrivini.

Robert Scrivini was invented by a man named Jon Santore (then a camp counselor of mine, now a decorated composer) and myself (then a boy, now an older boy) many years ago in North Carolina. We invented Scrivini because there were many occasions that called for fake people, particularly fake creative people. Who painted that painting, you know, the one I can't quite remember that shows a woman from the back standing by a window? Robert Scrivini, of course. What was the name of the mathematician who discovered the largest known prime? Robert Scrivini, of course. It started as a joke, like everything, like life itself, but eventually Scrivini became an all-purpose stand-in for every known type of creativity. Scrivini was a true original. He thought of everything. This achievement was enabled primarily by his nonexistence.

Pop music is filled with tangled cases of unoriginality: George Harrison's "My Sweet Lord" (1970), Puff Daddy's "I'll Be Missing You" (1997), Negativland. Scrivini shared my interest in pop songs that nearly replicate other pop songs. He even devised a devilish metaphor to explain the phenomenon. Do you know what *balut* is? It is a duck egg with a fertilized duck fetus inside of it. It is a Filipino snack food. The previous two sentences seem incompatible with one another, I know. Sorry. Both are true. "The pop balut," he writes, "occurs when one thing has another very similar thing inside of it, and the combination produces both appetite and the violent loss of appetite for both things." Scrivini reviews many cases of pop-chart baluts, for example, the Rolling Stones' "Under My Thumb," from the 1966 album *Aftermath*. A few years after that, I heard the Four Tops' 1965 single "It's the Same Old Song." My reaction was similar to the reaction Scrivini describes. I wanted to hear both songs again immediately, and then to never hear them again. The Stones had stolen from the Four Tops outright, and not only that, but stolen from a song that was itself about repetition and replaying. Scrivini has that insight as well: "The theft seems to encode its own confession (though it may have gone unnoticed by the band, which was later accused of copying the melody of k.d. lang's 'Constant Craving' for its 1997 song 'Anybody Seen My Baby?' and compelled to give a credit to lang and her cowriter, Ben Mink)." I put the Four Tops song on a mixtape called "Beforemath" as a form of reparation.

A few years later, when I heard Pee Wee Crayton's "Do Unto Others" (1954), I knew far more about the way that white British rockers stole from American bluesmen and early R&B singers. Led Zeppelin is the most obvious example. "Page, Plant and company would never have written a song if they didn't rewrite Bukka White, Sleepy John Estes, Memphis Minnie, and others," Scrivini writes. I disagree: They would have written only "The Song Remains the Same." I was prepared for any level of theft from Led Zeppelin, but other groups' borrowings were still capable of surprising me. Especially when they were so obvious: Crayton's opening blast of guitar was later, almost laughably, lifted wholesale by John Lennon for "Revolution." For some reason, I didn't mind this case as much. "Revolution" seemed like a better home for the stinging solo (here it appears in the version included on the 2006 album *Love*, which George Martin and his son Giles created for Cirque du Soleil). Revolutions, of course, are new things, but also complete rotations that return to the point of origin. Paul Gauguin said that "art is either plagiarism or revolution." He should have conceded that it can be both.

Scrivini, writing in the academic journal *Copy*, cites Crayton, and Lennon, and the Gauguin quote, but he is most satisfying when most obscure. At the height of disco, Rod Stewart released *Blondes Have More Fun*, an album that contained the monstrously popular "Da Ya Think I'm Sexy?" (1978). The song, of course, derailed (or maybe rerailed) Stewart's career, completing the transiton from sensitive singer-songwriter persona to cock-of-the-walk sex jester. "Da Ya Think I'm Sexy?" remains one of the best disco singles, as well as one of the easiest to parody. The problem is that it was already a parody. Five years earlier, Bobby Womack had released *Facts of Life*, the last of a string of classic early-seventies albums that included *Communication* and *Understanding*. The album fared somewhat poorly and helped send Womack into obscurity. But Rod Stewart heard the album, I'm sure, not just because the similarities are too glaring but because Stewart would certainly have followed Womack's career—Stewart was obsessed with Sam Cooke, the man who first signed Womack and his brothers to SAR Records in the early sixties, renaming them the Valentinos, and who employed Womack as a guitar player. (Speaking of taking what isn't exactly yours, Womack married Cooke's widow, Barbara, after Cooke's death.)

So what was Stewart thinking? Was the plagiarism unconscious? Was it an homage? Was it an attack against a powerful forebear in a time when he was fortuitously (or tragically) diminished? In the end, it registers as something oedipal, wonderful, and terrible, all at once. Scrivini, here, reaches for an original interpretation of Stewart's theft, and perhaps overreaches.

> Cultural eventfulness of the sort represented by Stewart's hit, which was literally "put on the floor" (read: under-foot) by a generation of dancers, offers a transformative under-standing of Womack that reenergizes Paolo Legno's Menardian reiteration of Edward Said's famous observation: "The best way to consider originality is to look not for first instances of a phenomenon, but rather to see duplication, parallelism, symmetry, parody, repetition, echoes of it. . . . The writer thinks less of writing originally, and more of rewriting."

The writer isn't the only one. The postmodernist feminist philosopher Millie Jackson combined the two songs into one medley on the 1979 live album *Live and Uncensored*. Millie Jackson has said most of the things that need to be said about relationships. She has said them over and over again. Why does she have to repeat herself? Because people don't listen—or at least don't listen closely.

24

CLICHÉ/INSPIRATION

BY THE LIGHT OF THE SILVERY MOON
Ada Jones – Single
Edison Blue Amberol: 1910

BY THE LIGHT OF THE SILVERY MOON
Jackie Wilson
Released 1957
Available on: *Mr. Excitement*
Rhino: 1992

MOON IN JUNE
Soft Machine – *Third*
Columbia: 1970

CRASH INTO JUNE
Game Theory – *The Big Shot Chronicles*
Enigma: 1986

EVENING IN JUNE
Van Morrison – *What's Wrong with This Picture?*
Blue Note: 2003

JUNE IS A FINE MONTH. KENYAN INDEPENDENCE. SUZI QUATRO'S BIRTH-day. Weddings. But in popular music, it has a reputation—a bad one. June, of course, is held up as one of the words that songwriters just shouldn't employ, and especially not in combination with certain celestial bodies and/or common utensils. Remember when Yoko Ono revealed that John Lennon would wake at night and worry about why people were covering Paul McCartney's songs rather than his? This was how she consoled him: "I used to tell him, 'It's because you are a talented songwriter. You don't just rhyme *June* with *spoon.*'"

You can argue she was being too hard on Paul, or that she was treating him fairly and being too hard on June. *June/moon/spoon* rhymes go back well before popular song, into romantic poetry, but they've been the cliché people use to disparage clichéd lyrics at least since the beginning of the last century. In 1915, in *Writing for Vaudeville*, Brett Page was already forgiving the sin as if it were universally familiar.

So far as the vital necessities of the popular song go, rhymes may occur regularly or irregularly, with fine effect in either instance, and the rhymes may be precise or not. To rhyme *moon* with *June* is not unforgivable.

Even so, it's hard to imagine that Page would entirely forgive "By the Light of the Silvery Moon." With music by Gus Edwards and lyrics by Edward Madden, the song was first published in 1908 and covered, over time, by nearly everyone: Doris Day, Gene Vincent, Fats Domino, Little Richard. Ada Jones did one of the oldest versions in 1910; Jackie Wilson did one of the most old-fashioned in 1957 (though with some truly crazy falsetto midway through). In any event, the lyrics leave no cliché turned.

> *By the light of the silvery moon*
> *I want to spoon*
> *To my honey, I'll croon love's tune*
> *Honey moon, keep a-shinin' in June*
> *Your silv'ry beams will bring love's dreams*
> *We'll be cuddlin' soon*
> *By the silvery moon*

The backlash came quickly. The Ring Lardner–George S. Kaufman play *June Moon* lampooned the songwriting business in 1929, and even before that, in 1921, the popular tenor Billy Murray, a frequent duet partner of Jones, recorded "Stand Up and Sing for Your Father an Old-Time Tune," which wished for a return to an era of emotional Irish ballads, before Tin Pan Alley had corroded the minds of youth.

Sure now, stand up and sing for your father an old-time
   tune
Please stop the trash that you sing
Morning, night, and noon
Oh, I'm sick of all those ditties
About moon and spoon and June
So will you stand up and sing for your father an old-time
   tune?

The distaste with the commonness of these rhymes has lasted a sur-prisingly long time, helped along by an explosion of lyrical imagination in the midsixties and the birth of hundreds of new clichés in the years since. In the Magnetic Fields' "With Whom to Dance?" (from *Get Lost*, all the way back in 1995), Stephin Merritt tries to have it both ways.

Moons in June—I've given up on that stuff
Arms have charms, but I've no hope of falling in love

Merritt may be rejecting hackneyed rhymes out of bitterness over being excluded from the corresponding experiences, but *he is reject-ing it*—the next rhyme pairs *dance* and *significance*. The better a song-writer, the thinking goes, the less likely he or she is to lean on *arms* and *charms*—or *love* and *dove*, or *heart* and *apart*, or *dream* and *seem*, or *fire* and *inspire*. *Moon* and *June* is simply the worst of a bad bunch. The critic and poet Clive James tried his hand as a lyricist in the seventies, in collaboration with the singer Pete Atkin. The resulting songs were complex and literary attempts—sometimes successful—to advance the form. In his poem "To Pete Atkin: A Letter from Paris," James lays the blame at the feet of pop music.

The Broadway partnership of words and tune
Had been dissolved by pop, which then reverted
In all good faith to rhyming moon with June
Well pleased with the banalities it blurted
Those speech defects would need attention soon

Soft Machine's "Moon in June" (1970) extends the argument even further, defiantly admitting a cliché into its title because its contents are so eclectic. And yet, underneath the thick blanket of prog rock, it's just a story about a man and a woman, though one sung with incomparable oddness by Robert Wyatt.

On a dilemma between what I need and what I just want
Between your thighs I feel a sensation
How long can I resist the temptation?

It may take more than ten minutes, but in the end, simplicity outs; the distance between "Moon in June" and, say, Wings' "Silly Love Songs" (1976) isn't as great as Wyatt (or Yoko Ono) might think.

Singing a song in the morning
Singing it again at night
Don't really know what I'm singing about
But it makes me feel all right

The song is clear that when something makes you feel all right, it doesn't need to be the source of too much scrutiny. While you can hold yourself apart from the clichés sometimes, at other times you have to submit. Game Theory's "Crash into June" frames its romance as jumpy and adolescent ("crash into June / in and out of tune / it happens all too soon"), and I've never been sure whether Scott Miller is singing about a girl, a summer night, or one in the other. Van Morrison's "Evening in June" (2003) opts for a wiser, warmer approach, more autumnal than summery.

> *By the light of the moon*
> *When the night holds the secrets of the sleepy lagoon*
> *I'm contemplating moonlight on the water*
> *When I'm walking with you on an evening in June*

Morrison has been on good terms with moons for nearly forty years, since "Moondance" at least, and he doesn't betray much anxiety about sinking into cliché. Or, for that matter, fretting over influence; the opening cushion of horns points directly to Joni Mitchell's "Car on the Hill," from 1974. But this is walking, not driving.

LONELINESS/COMPANY

BEN GREENMAN

GHOST IN MY HOUSE
Graham Parker
Recorded 1986
Available on: *Loose Monkeys*
UpYours: 1999

GONE
Ferlin Husky
Released 1957
Available on: *Greatest Hits*
Curb: 1990

MISS YOU SO
Lillian Offitt
Released 1957
Available on: *The Best of Excello Records*
Excello: 1994

HAVE YOU GONE
Mary Margaret O'Hara — *Apartment Hunting (Original Motion Picture Soundtrack)*
Outside: 2001

MISSING YOU
Diana Ross
Released 1984
Available on: *The Definitive Collection*
Hip-O: 2006

PLANS I MAKE
Hüsker Dü — *New Day Rising*
SST: 1985

A FEW YEARS BACK I WAS VACATIONING WITH MY FAMILY—MY PARENTS, my wife, my kids, nieces, nephews—and at the end of the first week, my wife, my younger son (he's three), and I returned to New York. My older son, who's six, stayed an extra week with my parents and his cousins. On the day we left, the three of us got onto a boat and waved at my older son, who was on the dock. "See you in seven days," he said, with a precision that betrayed his anxiety.

We returned to New York. For much of the next week, I went around the house in a fog. I had one kid there, but not both kids. The place was full of emptiness, haunted by it. I felt incomplete, and I tried to complete the picture. "So, are you homesick?" I said to my son when we spoke on the phone.

"Maybe a little," he said.

"Do you miss Brooklyn?"

"Yes." His voice wobbled slightly.

"Do you miss going to the park?"

"Yes." The wobbling increased.

At this point I was leading the witness. It wasn't that I wanted to break him down, exactly. But I did want to get a sense of what he was feeling about the separation. He's only six, of course, so I imagined that his feelings were more representative of some pure state, that he could admit them directly, without irony or defensiveness. Evidently I was wrong, because he recovered his composure. "Gotta go," he said. "There's a bat in the house."

During my son's week away, I had a number of other experiences of missing people, or maybe I was just tuned to that station. One friend of mine left for a long weekend in the Pacific Northwest with a friend of hers. They were having boring summers and thought that maybe the trip would reenergize them. Another old friend went abroad for the rest of the year. A third friend told me that he and his girlfriend were leaving New York for good. None of the departures was especially surprising. The friend in the first case always travels. The friend in the second case has spent a decent amount of her time out of the city—and some of that out of the country—for the last few years. The friend in the third case had discussed this move for the last six months. And yet, in every case, as soon as my friends told me about their trips, I began to miss them. It was difficult at first to understand why. For starters, it's not entirely appropriate to miss an adult friend. Or rather, you can miss anyone you want, but saying that you miss someone—or even acknowledging it to yourself—suggests a degree of emotional involvement that is, at the very least, untoward.

The world of pop music bears this out; the vast majority of songs about missing people are romantic songs. Take Graham Parker's excellent cover of R. Dean Taylor's "Ghost in My House" (1986), one of Motown's most durable rarities.

> There's a ghost in my house
> The ghost of your memories
> The ghost of the love you took from me

For two lines, this is a generic song, human to human. The third line blows all that up. Let's try again, with Ferlin Husky ("Gone," 1957).

> Since you've gone
> The moon, the sun, the stars in the sky
> Know the reason why I cry
> Love divine once was mine

For three lines, this might be platonic. I suppose you could be astronomically sad because your brother left Bakersfield. But it's not platonic. In "Miss You So" (1957), Lillian Offitt gets there even quicker, in the first word.

Darling, how I miss you
Oh, darling, how I miss you

In all these cases, what's emphasized is powerlessness. The songs suggest that there is not only a separation but an abandonment, that there is one party who has left and another who has been left behind. This sentiment is broadly inapplicable to my situations: With my son, I was the only potential abandoner, and with my friends, no one abandoned anyone. Adults were just living their lives, a process that sometimes brings them closer together and sometimes takes them farther apart. All these factors explained why I didn't say anything to my friends about anyone missing anyone else.

"Have a good trip." That I said. "Fly safe." That I said. "I'm sure Texas will be great." That I said.

But then, left to my own devices, I thought about this situation and the other, wondered at the weight of a departure. During my son's week away, I looked in his room, looked at his toys and books, spent time imagining the moment when he'd return. If anything, it served to remind me how much I enjoy him when he's around. As for my friends, the sense of being without was almost physical at first, more than a twinge if not quite an ache. I think maybe Mary Margaret O'Hara, writing (mostly) one of her singularly weird love songs ("Have You Gone," 2001), catches a piece of it.

I have no one to be anymore
You have no one to be anymore

When someone is nearby, in matter or in mind, you come to depend on that other person's presence to know that you are present. When they go, a piece of you may go with them. Identity, a fragile thing, cannot always endure the sudden shifts. And while with a child there is ultimate control—I can tell my son when to come home, and in fact he depends upon me to do so—with another adult there is an ultimate absence of control. In "Missing You" (1984), which Diana Ross recorded as a tribute to Marvin Gaye after his death, this is very clear. Written by Lionel Richie and based on conversations Richie had with Ross about Gaye, it plays like a straightforward lovelorn song.

> *Since you've been away I've been down and lonely*
> *Since you've been away I've been thinking of you*
> *Trying to understand the reason you left me*
> *What were you going through?*

Most lost-love songs at least hold out the faint hope of reunion. That's not the case here, even though the lyric won't admit it. There's a false optimism, both in the writing and in the lightness of the vocals, and this gives the song its bottomless sadness and a certain creepy beauty. It's a song of deep denial, more so than, say, Pink Floyd's "Wish You Were Here" (1975). And it's easy to understand why. People can walk toward you or away from you anytime they want. They can come and they can go at will—at *their* will. But the person who goes always has more power than the one who remains, whether it's in friendship, in love, or in death. Movement is less sad than the observation of motion.

CHILDHOOD/ADULTHOOD

QIDRECHINNA (I AM DESTINED TO LOVE)

Abdel Gadir Salim — *Blues in Khartoum*
Institute Du Monde Arabe: 1999

YA WANNA BUY A BUNNY?

Spike Jones and His City Slickers
Released 1949
Available on: *Greatest Hits!!!*
RCA: 1999

PINBALL WIZARD

Elton John — *Tommy: The Soundtrack*
Polydor: 1975

VALENTINE AND GARUDA

Frank Black and the Catholics — *Black Letter Days*
spinART: 2002

YOU'RE THE REASON OUR KIDS ARE UGLY

Conway Twitty and Loretta Lynn
Released 1978
Available on: *The Definitive Collection*
MCA Nashville: 2005

SEE THE BIG MAN CRY

Charlie Louvin
Released 1965
Available on: *Greatest Hits*
Collectors' Choice: 2004

When I was seven, I went through my parents' records and played all of them. It was a pretty standard midseventies set: Beatles, Beach Boys, Supremes, James Taylor, Carole King, *West Side Story*, maybe one or two Jimi Hendrix records. I remember sitting cross-legged in the living room and listening to Smokey Robinson.

I am using this memory as a shield against sentimentality.

Today is my older son's birthday. Last week was my younger son's birthday. My wife and I will throw them parties, take pictures, wish they had fewer toys: the usual. It's strange to have kids, especially kids who are becoming people, and it is also the most natural thing in the world.

I am using this truism as a shield against sentimentality.

There are few memories that still survive from the late seventies, when I was the age my children are now. It is mostly a blur of Jimmy Carter's gigantic teeth and TV commercials celebrating the bicentennial, principally through low rates on car loans. Still, I remember clearly the first time I heard Jim Croce's "One Less Set of Footsteps" (1973), and how frightened I was. I can't say exactly why, but the song terrified me then and still makes the hair on the back of my neck stand up today. I remember hearing the Ohio Players' "Love Rollercoaster" in 1975, when it was all over the radio, and trying to wiggle the blinds on one of the windows of my parents' living room to move in sync with the guitar part. So I don't want to underestimate the degree to which my sons, even if they're not identifying themselves by the music they like, are identifying music that they like.

My younger son seems, so far, to favor soundtrack music and classical music, neither of which made a tremendous impression on my older son when he was that age. When we watch movies, my younger son will start humming the score and say, "I like this music." Later on, he will hum it again. My older son prefers songs with simple melodies and complicated lyrics. He repeats the lyrics to himself later. The earliest examples of this, which date from when he was two or even younger, are Ian Dury's "Sex and Drugs and Rock and Roll" (1977), Captain Beefheart's "Tropical Hot Dog Night" (1978), and Frank Black's "Valentine and Garuda" (2002). I'd be playing them at home or in the car and he'd perk up, and ask me what they were, and smile, and laugh, and ask for them again. There are enough exceptions, of course, that these cease to be rules. The younger one got completely hooked on the Hives' "Tick Tick Boom" (2007). The older one loves Buddy Holly. The younger one once forced me, for twenty nights in a row, to put him to bed with a copy of "Born in the U.S.A." (1984) playing in an old cassette machine that was very similar to one I had in 1976. The older one, at three, choreographed a modern dance set to Elton John's version of "Pinball Wizard" (1975). He later taught it to the younger one, who added a few flourishes of his own. Both of them worship Michael Jackson and AC/DC and Spike Jones, which only means that they are part of the human race. And both of them are obsessed to the point of joy with "Qidrechinna" (1999), a song by the Sudanese pop singer Abdel Gadir Salim.

I am writing this when they are young knowing that they will, as soon as I stop writing it, get older. They will cease to experience that joy, or they will conceal that joy from me and my wife. That day's not too far off. Until then, they're little, and their appetite for the world is large, and so I'm going to wish them a happy birthday with a quartet of songs that they love, and then a pair of songs that they don't know. The new gifts are country songs, because it's a genre they don't particularly like, and I am a sadist. I am using sadism as a shield against sentimentality. One of them is Loretta Lynn and Conway Twitty's "You're the Reason Our Kids Are Ugly" (1978), which distills the chaos of domestic bliss into low comedy.

> *Besides that, all of our kids took after your part of our*
> * family anyway*
> *Oh they did, huh? What about the ones that's bald?*
> *Well, I guess you might say they took after me*

I am using low comedy as a shield against sentimentality.

The other is Charlie Louvin's "See the Big Man Cry" (1965), in which a man spies on his estranged wife and the child who does not even know him. Many married men have imagined circumstances that would separate them from their wives—falling in love with others, losing the war of attrition against boredom and self-hatred. Many men have imagined surviving that transition. But being separated from children is an atrocity, and Louvin mines it for maximum horror.

> *I followed them to a pet shop window the little boy stopped*
>   *to see*
> *He looked up at her, said If I had a daddy, he'd buy that*
>   *puppy for me.*

I am using horror as a shield against sentimentality.

I am not, as you will notice, including Harry Chapin's "Cat's in the Cradle" (1974), though I will admit that *Verities and Balderdash*, the album on which the song originally appeared, was one of the records in my parents' collection, and that I probably took it out and played it once or twice. I am not posting it because, well, I am still holding the shield against sentimentality, though it's quaking a little bit when I think of my sons, littler than I ever remember being, loving music without the slightest bit of irony.

NOVELTY/CONVENTION

TRANSFUSION

Nervous Norvus
Released 1956
Available on: *Stone Age Woo: The Zorch Sounds of Nervous Norvus*
Norton: 2004

NOON BALLOON TO RANGOON

Nervous Norvus
Released 1956
Available on: *Stone Age Woo: The Zorch Sounds of Nervous Norvus*
Norton: 2004

WHAT ARE FRIENDS FOR IF YOU DON'T ANSWER THEIR COMPLAINTS? I have a friend whose recent past is a pileup of bad decisions. She would be the first to admit it. Very recently, though, she has made a number of good choices. She is more stable than ever. But sometimes there are still poor moods. There was one recently, and there didn't seem to be a reason. Her new boyfriend was treating her wonderfully. She had just gotten a raise at work. The weather was nice. "Maybe it's just me," she said. "Maybe I'm too restless."

"How so?"

"You know," she said. "I think maybe I like novelty too much."

We hung up, and I thought about what she said, because, well, it's interesting. Does she like novelty too much? Life is boring at times—that seems hard to dispute—and while that boredom can be a source of frustration, it can also be a source of motivation. If you're in a job that has ceased to engage you, find a new one or a way to make the old one work. If you're in a relationship that feels drab, rejuvenate yourself within it or rejuvenate yourself without it. But the process of making things new is sometimes difficult to manage without feeling like a spoiled and greedy child. When you're seeking out new stimuli, how do you know when the jolt you've found is genuinely contributing to your sense of self and to the progress of your life (and when you're genuinely contributing to the lives of others), or if it's merely a new blip whose intensity will soon fade, leaving you yet again in search of something new? Should you settle for boring things and look for excitement in other areas of your life, or should you hold out hope that you will discover something that exactly matches your needs?

These are only random notes on the problem, not even a whole melody. But thinking about novelty led me to thinking about novelty songs. The term, of course, refers to songs that are noteworthy not primarily for the beauty of their music or the skill of their musicians or the passion of their vocals, but rather for their comic strangeness. Sheb Wooley's "The Purple People Eater" (1958) is one of the most famous novelty songs in the history of novelty songs. "They're Coming to Take Me Away, Ha-Haaa!" (1966) by Napoleon XIV is another. It's annoying. On the other hand, there's C. W. McCall's "Convoy" (1975), which has the power to warm even the coldest hearts, and there are dozens of novelty-flavored songs by artists with broader, more legitimate careers, such as Randy Newman's "Short People" (1977), Todd Rundgren's "Bang the Drum All Day" (1982), and the Offspring's "Pretty Fly (For a White Guy)" (1998).

Novelty songs provide respite from the drudgery of life, like a juggler appearing at work. But which juggler do you prefer? The guy dressed like a jester? The one who adds an apple in with his juggling balls and takes a bite of it when it comes around? This is a highly personal choice. I once dated a girl who loved Cheech and Chong's "Earache My Eye" (1974), no matter how many times I'd try to redirect her to Spike Jones. I'm sure some of you even know people who like Ray Stevens's "The Streak" (1974). When they get out of jail, you can ask them why.

Even in the land of novelty songs, there are flares of genius. Jimmy Drake was working as a truck driver in the midfifties when he began to make records under the name Nervous Norvus. Over the course of a year, he recorded a string of truly cracked songs that mixed absurdist jive (much borrowed from the Bay Area musician and DJ Red Blanchard), conversational singing (with occasional leaps into strangulated yowling), and highly rudimentary guitar backing (supplemented by sound effects).

Drake's first hit as Nervous Norvus, "Transfusion" (1956), sketches a series of car wrecks, focusing on (as the title indicates) the sanguinary needs of the victims. It belongs to the fairly large genre of car crash songs ("Leader of the Pack," "Last Kiss," "Tell Laura I Love Her"), but it's also a novelty song about novelty—all the crashes are caused by speeding, and all require (literally and metaphorically) new blood. There are parts of "Transfusion" that could come from a love song, or at least a lust song.

> *Transfusion transfusion*
> *My red corpsucles [sic] are in mass confusion*

The transfusion requests are the heart of the song: They end each verse with absurd rhymes—"Slip the blood to me, Bud," "Shoot the juice to me, Bruce," "Pass the claret to me, Barrett," and, best, "Pass the crimson to me, Jimson"—that forecast Paul Simon's "50 Ways to Leave Your Lover" (1975), another song about finding new blood. There's a tension, though, because the thrill of recklessness is counterweighted by risk.

> *I'm never never never gonna speed again*

But he does. He always does.

"Transfusion," which went top ten, was followed by "Ape Call" (1956), a consideration of the courting practices of cavemen, and then there was one more Nervous Norvus single, "The Fang" (1956), a story about a Martian who comes to earth to chase skirt. But commercial momentum was slowing, in part because Drake didn't like appearing live as Nervous Norvus—he turned down a chance to perform "The Fang" on *The Ed Sullivan Show*—and soon the act was history. Drake died in 1968.

Then, in 2004, Norton Records released a compilation that included several outtakes, including "Noon Balloon to Rangoon" (1956), which had been rediscovered in a thrift store in Oakland and found its way back to the airwaves courtesy of Dr. Demento. "Noon Balloon to Rangoon" isn't just an oddity—it's a masterful oddity that holds up as one of the finest Nervous Norvus offerings. It shares most of the melody of "Transfusion," such as it is, and like its predecessor, it is a meta-novelty song. The lyrics are drawn directly from The Thousand and One Nights, perhaps literature's greatest lesson in the lifesaving powers of novelty.

> *Nervous Ali-Baba was a zorch mahalt*
> *He trapped the forty thieves and laughed to hear them*
> *   shout*
> *What became of Ali-Baba when the thieves got out?*
> *Noon balloon to Rangoon*

The lyrics go on, through Sinbad, through Scheherezade, but just as in "Transfusion" there's a tension between stimulus and safety.

> *Rangoon is the safest place when you get in a jam*
> *So don't be a goon 'round about noon*
> *Take that balloon and scram, Sam.*

The balloon is a vehicle of escape, but look at the escape route—it's to Rangoon, the "safest place" (it's not, by the way, but maybe Nervous Norvus was looking at different statistics). Is that the solution, to pursue novelty from a solid foundation? And would Rangoon be deadly dull (rather than "a safe retreat") without the magic of the lamp or the carpet? It's worth further study. I'm not saying that all the answers to the questions of restlessness, energy, intensity, and comfort—how long to hold a job, how long to keep a lover, how long to stay in one place before hopping on a train or a plane or into a balloon—reside in two minutes of a never-released song recorded by a virtually unknown novelty singer. But I'm not saying that they're not.

CRAZINESS/SANITY

SOME PEOPLE ARE CRAZY
John Martyn — *Grace and Danger*
Antilles: 1980

BABY'S CRAZY
Larry Williams
Recorded 1958
Available on: *At His Finest: The Specialty Rock 'N' Roll Years*
Ace: 2004

CRAZY WOMAN
Bill Wyman — *Monkey Grip*
Rolling Stones / Atlantic: 1974

DON'T BE CRAZY
John Lennon
Demo recorded circa 1975

8 TON CRAZY
Andy Fairweather Low — *La Booga Rooga*
A&M: 1975

RETURN OF THE CRAZY ONE
Digital Underground — *The Body-Hat Syndrome*
Tommy Boy: 1993

I CALLED MY WIFE CRAZY THIS WEEK. SHE DESERVED IT. OBJECTIVELY speaking, for a little while at least, she was every kind of loon. I wouldn't say *flibbertigibbet*, because that's sexist. I wouldn't say *murderer*, because that's inaccurate. I'd say *crazy*. When I said it, though, she recoiled at the word. "Why don't you leave me alone?" she said. She should have thanked me. A crazy person has hundreds of songs at her disposal to clarify and celebrate her condition. In fact, you can argue that it's one of the five or six most decorated words in the history of pop music. Sounds crazy, I know.

The most common use of crazy is romantic: Patsy Cline's "Crazy," Billie Holiday's "I've Got a Man, He's Crazy for Me," Chet Baker's "You're Driving Me Crazy (What Did I Do?)," and Fine Young Cannibals' "She Drives Me Crazy," to name just a few. In others, it's just a way of expressing energy: Prince's "Let's Go Crazy" or, for that matter, the Clash's earlier song of the same name. But then there are the songs that investigate a darker, richer seam of meaning, where crazy means what crazy means: a temporary loss of reason due to a combination of emotional and psychological factors.

That's the case in "Some People Are Crazy" (1980), one of the signature songs of the British singer-songwriter John Martyn. I missed Martyn the first time he passed through my life, in college, when a slightly older guy I knew insisted that he was like Eric Clapton but with brains. "But that's not like Eric Clapton at all!" I said, and we both had a hearty laugh, and I went on my way. In the last year or two, I have found my way back to Martyn, or he has found his way back to me, thanks largely to his 1980 album *Grace and Danger*. The record can sound smooth and jazzy if you don't pay close attention, but beneath the surface it's as raw a dissection of a failing relationship as, say, Richard and Linda Thompson's *Shoot Out the Lights*. "Some People Are Crazy," the opener, isn't among the most bruising songs on the record. At first blush, it seems like another "crazy for" song, another song about how lost love can drive a man to distraction, but as it goes on, it becomes clear that there's a broader brief.

> *Some people are crazy*
> *Some people are just plain good*
> *Some people talk wouldness and couldness*
> *Some people don't do as they should*

There's more taxonomy at work here. Some people are just plain good? Is that a form of craziness? Is resistance to plain goodness a necessary personal evolution? One of the people who didn't do as he should was Larry Williams. Williams started out as a songwriter and performer at Specialty Records in the midfifties, and he was designated as the label's star when Little Richard left rock and roll for the ministry in 1957. Williams had the songs, like "Bony Moronie" (1957) and "Dizzy Miss Lizzy" (1958). He had the style. He had the platform. In "Baby's Crazy" (1958), though, he may be grasping at straws—his main piece of evidence against the woman in the song, Marie, is that she doesn't love him like she used to do. Maybe she just came to her senses, or moved on. In real life, Williams's problems were more severe than just missing out on the record hop, thanks largely to his involvement with pimping and dealing. His life in the sixties and seventies was marked by drug and gun trouble, and in 1980 he was found dead of a gunshot wound outside of his Laurel Canyon home in a highly suspicious suicide.

Guns also figure in Bill Wyman's solo work, though they seem the stuff of blues legend rather than of reality. *Monkey Grip*, the bassist's 1974 album, was the first solo product from a Rolling Stone, and it opens with "I Wanna Get Me a Gun," which featured an excellent piano solo by Dr. John. "Crazy Woman" is the second song. The woman in the song catches the man with someone, and flies into a fury. That seems reasonable, but the song then accelerates quickly, in the sense that it returns to the album's first song.

> *Crazy woman*
> *She said I'm gonna get what's coming*
> *Crazy woman*
> *Gonna get me with a gun*

Wyman's song highlights the ways in which *crazy* can be used as dismissal, even if it's tinged with admiration. After all, who is more qualified to offer his opinion on a woman's mental fitness than Wyman, who began a relationship with Mandy Smith when he was forty-seven and she was thirteen, and who drove her to a nervous breakdown and anorexia?

I'll end with a plea for sanity from John Lennon—"Don't Be Crazy," from the Dakota demos, is Lennon's workup for "(Just Like) Starting Over" (1980). It's just a fragment, with placeholder lyrics. "Why don't they leave us alone?" he asks. "I cannot fill your empty life for you." But that's not true, at least not where my wife is concerned. Lennon is her favorite singer. He has already helped to fill her life, and it is far from empty. When my wife first heard the fragment, she told me that she thought it was superior to "(Just Like) Starting Over." "It has more mystery in it," she says. "It's harder to figure out, which makes it more satisfying."

At first, I laughed at this idea. How could it be better than one of his finest songs? Now I am sure she is right. I told her so. "I know that I'm right," she said. "I'm not crazy." Who said she was?

LEARNING/UNLEARNING

BEN GREENMAN

THE DARK PAGES OF SEPTEMBER LEAD TO THE NEW LEAVES OF SPRING
Paul Weller — *22 Dreams*
Yep Roc / Island: 2008

MY PHILOSOPHY
Boogie Down Productions — *By All Means Necessary*
Jive: 1988

OKWUKWE NA NCHEKWUBE
Celestine Ukwu and His Philosophers National
Released 1974
Available on: *Nigeria Special: Modern Highlife, Afro-Sounds & Nigerian Blues, 1970–6*
Soundway: 2008

PHILOSOPHY
Them
Released 1965
Available on: *The Story of Them Featuring Van Morrison*
Deram: 1997

SHIT FROM AN OLD NOTEBOOK
Minutemen — *Double Nickels on the Dime*
SST: 1984

THIS SUMMER, LIKE EVERY SUMMER, I PASSED THROUGH A MONTHLONG stretch where my reading was split almost exactly between crime fiction and philosophy. Wait—let me rearrange that so that the adjective doesn't look distributive. I passed through a stretch where my reading was split almost exactly between philosophy and crime fiction. Not philosophy fiction! Damn it! I mean actual philosophy: Kierkegaard, Hegel, Wittgenstein, Plato. The crime fiction is easy to explain. In summer, there is time on the beach. Procedurals and thrillers are printed in mass-market sizes. They fit easily in pockets. Plus, you can read them fast.

192

The philosophy is trickier. I still have my old books from college and grad school. But when I read philosophy, I rarely crack them open. That's because there's a deeper, shallower reason for needing philosophy at this time of year. I spend most of my time dealing with books: books as products, books as organs, books as bribes and tail feathers and millstones. I write books myself and publish them, as do a(n) (alarmingly) large percentage of my friends. Philosophy can take place in a book, but just as often it takes place in a text. Free philosophy writings, which you can have by the bushel for your Kindle, have summer portability, but that's the least of their powers. They open up a magical door through which I can escape this world, the book world, for a moment, while still getting from it what I need. I can't tell you the number of times that I have been standing in bookstores, looking at this shelf or that table, and that I have started to feel queasy, unable to abide the thought of the latest novel by Writer I Know or the latest memoir by Writer Someone Else I Know Knows. Another book by another person in the neighborhood or someone in an identical neighborhood elsewhere: yecch. "Yecch" is an uncharitable thought, or at least an uncomfortable one. It doesn't settle easily. But it's true, and that's what philosophy texts are for, right? I (try to) read philosophy because I need to step in many directions at once: to step back into what I perceive as an unreachable past, to step upward into what I perceive as a zone of broader truth, and most of all to step sideways out of the line of fire.

Normally, this would be the point where I would outline some of what I have learned from philosophy and some of what I hope to learn. I might mention Lyotard or Aristotle or the Symparanekromenoi, as unpretentiously as possible, which isn't really unpretentious at all. But I'm not going to do that. I'm not a philosopher, by training or by temperament. I have friends who are. They are programmatic for long stretches. They work through the texts at hand. While they are mastering them methodically, they are storing up energy. Then, all at once, they make an intuitive or a moral or an analytical leap. That's how new philosophy is made and how the case is advanced. I don't work that way, which is to say that I don't work at all, not as a philosopher. I skip around. I master single sentences or paragraphs but leave the rest to chance. It's hard not to think of that line from *A Fish Called Wanda*, when Kevin Kline, as the crazy Otto, responds to being called an ape by saying "apes don't read philosophy" and receives the all-time greatest rejoinder.

"Yes they do," Jamie Lee Curtis says. "They just don't understand it."

Since I am, apelike, crippled by poor training and poor temperament, I'm just going to say that reading philosophy comforts me via worthy removal from the moment. I'm not reading these philosophy texts to understand books better, but because I understand them as something different (better) than books. It's only one way of dealing with the material, but it's my way. As KRS-One says:

> *This is just one style, out of many*
> *Like a piggy bank, this is one penny*

One of the problems, I think, is that it's too easy to come to see books as products, partly because they are products. Authors love/hate to talk about sales because they love/hate what sales represent: acceptance of their ideas, of their core. But the truth is that sales mean nothing in a historical sense. Some of the books we read now as classics of the canon were busts during their authors' lifetimes. Some of the books that were huge hits have vanished from sight. You can make (and I have made) the argument that there is in fact an inverse relationship between time-local sales and time-global relevance: Anything that seems to matter so much at the moment is not built to last, and while this is reassuring, it is also sophistic (meaning plausible but fallacious; see: I have been reading philosophy).

But the other thing is undeniably true. You just don't know which books will matter later, and how much they'll matter. This is why making books is an exciting and sickening process. Your vogue could peak during your lifetime. It could be sparked again by a critic making a discovery in 2019, or 2025, or never. Still, it is important to remember that there is no real correlation between numbers and value: Never has been, never will be. Books may be products with covers and endcaps and tie-ins, but what is inside them is not. For me, philosophy books are especially genuine endeavors: While philosophers, when alive, are certainly just as subject to these endcap and tie-in anxieties as any author, their books seem to lend themselves better to de-booking. Innards can be brought out and allowed to speak for themselves. Product can give way to productivity. This is a borderline preachy point, which is why I'll let the Minutemen make it for me.

> *Let the products sell themselves*
> *Fuck advertising and commercial psychology*

Are the Minutemen speaking about all products? Does their notion of product include pop songs themselves? And what does it mean for a product to sell itself? As with all good philosophy, the questions asked are not fully answered.

30

PUBLICITY/PRIVACY

BEN GREENMAN

YOUNGER POINT OF VIEW
The Dogs
Released 1976
Available on: *DIY: We're Desperate—The L.A. Scene (1976–1979)*
Rhino: 1993

TEENAGE PRESIDENT TALKING BLUES
Kim Fowley – *Hotel Insomnia*
Marilyn: 1992

THIS STORY STARTS WITH TWO BEAUTIFUL WOMEN. I KNEW NEITHER OF
them. I know neither of them. It was on the subway. One was black,
tall, and to my left. One was short, white, and to my right. Both were
around twenty. It made for a nice balance, which isn't to say symmetry.
I am old and married and still I ogled: nature's way, for a minute. Then
I got on with noticing other things, including that both were reading
books, one of which was *The Secret History* and the other of which was
The Man Who Mistook His Wife for a Hat.

Despite the beauty, despite the youth, despite it all, I wasn't ogling
anymore. I was rereading, or at least remembering reading. *The Man
Who Mistook His Wife for a Hat* came out in 1985, when I was in high
school. *The Secret History* came out in 1992, after I was out of college. I
can't prove this, but I think that I read more books during those seven
years than in any other seven-year period in my life. This doesn't mean
that I read with any goal in mind other than the reading itself, or that
I retained very much of what I read, or that I was able to connect the
books I read to specific emotions or events in my life. It just means
that I went through a book a day, sometimes two, friction burns on
the pads of my thumbs. I read like it was going out of style, which it
was: I couldn't have known it at the time, but a few years after that my
pace slowed. It's only gotten worse. I can still rip through a new novel
on the subway ride home, but I don't consider it reading. I consider it

watching TV on the page. Reading now takes time. It requires losing the thread and then picking it up again. It requires ambition, thwarted and then (hopefully) achieved. Now, a book goes into me over a half week of stolen hours.

I'm off track. The subway stayed on track. The beautiful women stayed on the subway. My thoughts stayed on the beautiful women. I watched them for another minute—nature's way—and then I started thinking more about the books they were reading. The second phase of my thinking was significantly more superficial than the first. I had read both of those books, long ago. Been there, done that. I felt a half second of superiority and then a much longer period of something else, maybe the opposite. The careful case I had built for setting aside greedy, promiscuous reading for a more carefully curated selection dissolved, and what was left was the sense that youth had passed, all at once. It was wrong to be ogling twenty-year-olds and it was sad that they were discovering books that were long since dead to me, and while it was probably true that a sixty-year-old woman was looking at me and thinking the same thing, that was no consolation.

Time passes. It passes you. There is no way to remove the venom from this truism. This is the case with music even more powerfully than with books. The years of discovery end with a thud and we become conservationists, at least most of us. The Dogs, who came out of Lansing, Michigan, when the Stooges were tearing up Detroit and spent the seventies moving between punk pop and pop punk, explained this so perfectly that all I have to do is quote them, which is to say remember them, because I heard them first when I was young, and you don't forget those things.

> I seen Chicago on the TV yesterday, didn't make Woodstock
> Seen all the children of love fade away . . .
> With a younger point of view

The subway stayed on track. One of the women put away her book and took out a magazine. Barack Obama was on the cover, along with Hillary Clinton's name. Time passes. It passes you. This is the case with politics as powerfully as with music or books. The Dogs understood that, too: They were as political a pop-punk band as you were likely to find, picking up the thread not only from the Stooges but from the MC5. We have years of intense receptivity and then years of trying to make sense of what we received.

The other night I saw a documentary on Helen Thomas, the late, great grande dame of White House press coverage. What struck me as startling was the way that she became more liberal, more convinced of the importance of taking a strong stance against the evasions of the powerful, as she got older. This isn't the usual way. Usually progress through the world contextualizes passions, fits them in alongside realities, removes sharp edges. Obama looked old on the cover of the magazine. Obama once looked so young. The women on the subway looked so young. Did Obama matter more to them than he does to me?

Kim Fowley is older than you think, if you think of him at all. He's so old that he's no longer with us. Before he died in the summer of 2015, he wrote and produced hundreds of songs, including "Teenage President Talking Blues" (1992). The title of the album is probably stolen from a book by the poet Charles Simic. Fowley, of course, was a known cultural provocateur and Svengali, an inappropriate appropriator responsible for, among other things, the novelty hit "Alley Oop" (1960) and the novelty band the Runaways. "Teenage President Talking Blues" is odd, like nearly everything Fowley recorded. It describes a young man's arrival in Hollywood in 1959. I don't think it's autobiographical, exactly, because Fowley, the son of a Hollywood character actor, was already there; he had worked at American International and Arwin Records and was well on his way to novelty-song fame. In the song, the young man comes to Hollywood and promptly sets about making a spectacle of himself.

With silk underwear and platform shoes
I'm limber like a lady I hang real loose
I dress to kill and am ready to rock
I've got legs like a ladder and hands just like a clock

I watched the women on the subway. One of them noticed, met my gaze, dropped her gaze. That's youth, isn't it? Wonderful to look at and wondering if anyone is looking, needful of attention but also of enough anonymity and freedom to read, listen, see, try, and eventually to grow into something older, something else.

More people boarded. They interfered with my clean lines of sight. The two girls and their books must have had earlier stops, because by the time I got to Midtown they were gone. The one who had been reading the magazine had left it on the seat. I felt young remembering when Obama looked young, in Chicago, years before. This isn't a satisfying piece about youth and age. This isn't a satisfying piece about books. This isn't a satisfying piece about politics. This isn't a satisfying piece about people. Is it ever possible to bring those things into sharp focus, to fix them, or do they escape as quickly as they're acquired, forcing you to go back to them? I don't know, but I mean to find out. Nature's way.

BEGINNINGS/ENDS

BEN GREENMAN

I'M BEGINNING TO SEE THE LIGHT
Duke Ellington and His Orchestra
Released 1944
Available on: *The Complete RCA Victor Mid-Forties Recordings (1944–1946)*
RCA Victor: 2000

I'M BEGINNING TO SEE THE LIGHT
Duke Ellington and Louis Armstrong
Recorded 1961
Available on: *The Great Summit: The Master Takes*
Roulette Jazz / Blue Note: 2000

BEGINNING TO SEE THE LIGHT
The Velvet Underground — *The Velvet Underground*
MGM: 1969

BEGINNING TO SEE THE LIGHT (live)
The Velvet Underground
Recorded 1969
Available on: *The Legendary Guitar Amp Tapes* (bootleg)

IN THE BEGINNING GOD
Duke Ellington
Released 1966
Available on: *The Duke Ellington Centennial Edition: The Complete RCA Victor Recordings (1927–1973)*
RCA Victor: 1999

WANNA BE STARTIN' SOMETHIN'
Michael Jackson — *Thriller*
Epic: 1982

WANNA BE STARTIN' SOMETHIN' 2008
Michael Jackson featuring Akon — *Thriller 25*
Epic/Legacy: 2008

204

DON'T STOP THE MUSIC
Rihanna — *Good Girl Gone Bad*
Def Jam / SRP: 2007

It's December 31. There's champagne on the table. There are hats on heads. Happy New Year. If it is not December 31, consider this an exercise. Along with the celebration, there's a complaint: The beginning of a year is such an illusion that it's almost not worth remarking upon. The same disappointments that were present on December 31 are present on January 1. The problems that were on the table on December 31 are still on the table on January 1. The same events that were current on December 31 are current on January 1. The only thing that begins as the new year dawns is hope, and since it's traveling by itself, it is, by definition, false hope.

I have a friend who called me to compare our New Year's Eve parties. Hers was okay, she said. Her skirt was very short. She then told me that she was drawing up a list of goals for the new year, making a point of alternating between substantial resolutions (be a better person; renew faith in faith) and trivial ones (return to very short skirt with some regularity). I said I might jot down some resolutions, but I won't, unless they start with "Don't make any more resolutions," and that's a cheap ticket.

Though I don't think the new year starts anything, I am well aware of the importance of fresh starts. Without them, it's all middle or end, and that's hard to endure. So where are the real beginnings? There's Hüsker Dü's "New Day Rising" (1985) or the Breeders' "New Year" (1993), although they're kind of generic, one in a revolutionary key, one in a pantheistic one. I was thinking of something more specific, and that's how I found my way to Duke Ellington's "I'm Beginning to See the Light" (1944), a song about the genesis of romantic awareness.

I never cared much for moonlit skies
I never wink back at fireflies
But now that the stars are in your eyes
I'm beginning to see the light

The song was composed by Ellington and Johnny Hodges and fitted to lyrics by Don George and Harry James. It was one of the first records that Ellington made after the lifting of the American Federation of Musicians' recording ban, which was called in August 1942 as a result of the union's belief that mechanical reproduction of records was ruining the careers of performing musicians. Record companies were asked to pay royalties to the union, and eventually did—Decca relented in September 1943, followed closely by Capitol, and a year after that by Columbia and Victor. Recording artists had a new beginning, and Ellington was eager to set down a version of the already-popular song. He did, with vocals from Joya Sherrill—soon enough, he was joined by nearly every other performer of standards, from James (his version charted higher than Ellington's) to Ella Fitzgerald to the Ink Spots to Bobby Darin. Louis Armstrong took a crack at it when he and Ellington recorded together in 1961, and he turned in a brilliant vocal that is, typically, both earthy and empyrean.

Within a decade, the title of the song, and some of its sense, had migrated from jazz to rock. The late Lou Reed's lyric quickly points to an epiphany that is at once broader and deeper.

Some people work very hard, but still they never get it right
Well, I'm beginning to see the light

As it rolls along, it sidesteps the difficulties of modern existence ("there are problems in these times / But—woo!—none of them are mine") before breaking euphorically into its predecessor's space: "How does it feel to be loved?" The second version is an instrumental, sort of: It's from the Legendary Guitar Amp tapes (1969), which were the result of a tech at the Boston Tea Party club plugging his recorder directly into Lou Reed's amplifier. It's very difficult (and very foolish) to say that one Velvet Underground song is the best, but in certain moods, such as the mood produced by the false beginning of a new year, this is the best.

Locating new beginnings within light and light within love isn't a bad idea, but it has its limits. Duke Ellington, later on, located some of those limits with his aggressive exploration of faith and devotion. These were his Sacred Concerts, the first of which premiered in San Francisco's Grace Cathedral in September 1965. The centerpiece of that first Sacred Concert was the first piece, "In the Beginning God," a twenty-minute epic that starts with a piano solo, gives way to a baritone-saxophone solo by Harry Carney, begins to move with the power you might expect needed for a Genesis—whose first four words, of course, give the piece its title—and then arrives at a fleet, jivey monologue by Brock Peters that sounds like the precursor to Chuck D's "No" (1996).

No limit, no budget
No bottom, no topless
No cows, no bulls
No barracuda, no buffalo
No birds, no bees, no beetles

Or is it *Beatles*? Ellington began to write the text after he learned that Billy Strayhorn, his collaborator for nearly thirty years, was dying of cancer. Maybe he was making a stand for jazz against rock and roll, which must have seemed like a new beginning at the time, or a novelty, or a step backward, depending on who you were.

You can begin to see the light. You can try to see God's first light. You can work very hard and try to get it right. These are all useful ways of exposing the artificiality of the new year, although the meaninglessness of arbitrary beginnings already has an anthem, and an excellent one at that: Michael Jackson's "Wanna Be Startin' Somethin'" (1982). It's a song about gossip, give or take.

> *Billie Jean is always talkin'*
> *When nobody else is talkin'*
> *Tellin' lies and rubbin' shoulders*
> *So they called her mouth a motor*

Anyone who doesn't think Michael Jackson is one of the two or three finest singers in pop music history should listen to the way he sings "So they called her mouth a motor." But then listen to the rest of the song, and realize that it rapidly and intentionally devolves into a song about how gossip is not only malignant but meaningless, and not just gossip, but everything else: existence, maybe, when you're stuck in the middle and the pain is thunder. The final resolution of the problem, when he decides to lift his "head up high, and scream out to the world 'I know I am someone,' and let the truth unfurl," is a nice sentiment, until it, too, devolves into nonsense: "mamase mamasa mamakossa." (Of course, it's not really nonsense. It's the chant from Manu Dibango's "Soul Makossa," from 1972, but here it's nonsense, and the best kind.)

Twenty-five years after Jackson released the album that started with "Wanna Be Startin' Somethin'" (it was called *Thriller*—you may have heard of it), the record industry tried to squeeze more blood out of the stone by rereleasing it with five special modern remixes. Here's the thing about special modern remixes: They are usually so bad that calling them terrible is insulting to terrible things. Most of these are no exception. Kanye West redid "Billie Jean," somehow subtracting all that's exciting about the song, which is pretty much the entire song. Fergie defanged "Beat It." Will.i.am applied some wit.less.ness to "The Girl Is Mine." The only version that didn't qualify as a botched plastic surgery was Akon's remix/remake of "Wanna Be Startin' Somethin'" (2008), which transforms the song from a battle challenge to a bedroom come-on. It was smooth and seductive and even a little bit menacing. And it's not the best remix of the material. That would be Rihanna's "Don't Stop the Music," which was something else entirely, an original song and a derivative song and a propulsive song and a great song. It lit the wick of *Thriller* all over again. How do you make great things great again? Relight them. It delights them.

A little more than a year after the record company injured *Thriller* while pretending to improve it, Michael Jackson died. I was in a corner grocery with my children. A woman in the back of the store was crying. "He's gone," she said. For some reason (maybe there was music on in the background, or maybe we were just participating in some collective grief), we knew immediately who she meant. "He didn't," my younger son said, because what would you do when plunged into darkness but try to turn on the light? "Please don't stop the music," my older son sang quietly, to himself, to all of us.

Six months after that, we celebrated New Year's. It was the first year I let them stay up until midnight. We played only Michael Jackson songs. One of the songs was "Speechless," from his last studio album, *Invincible*. It's a song about wonder that Jackson was inspired to write, supposedly, after a water-balloon fight with children in Germany. I can't speak to the legal wisdom of that particular activity, but I can say that the song brought both of my children to the brink of tears. Partly, that's because the lyrics are nowhere near as simply joyous as Jackson himself seems to believe. There's one line in particular that seemed to shine more brightly than the others, but bright in the fashion of eyes wet with tears: "When I'm with you, I am in the light where I cannot be found." The year ended. The last year in which Michael Jackson was alive on earth ended. We celebrated the new year. He remained in the light where he could not be found.

SILENCE/CONVERSATION

QUIET MAN
John Prine — *John Prine*
Atlantic: 1972

SO QUIET IN HERE
Van Morrison — *Enlightenment*
Mercury: 1990

THE QUIET ONE
The Who — *Face Dances*
Warner Bros.: 1981

QUIETLY
Fred Eaglesmith — *Tinderbox*
Lonesome Day: 2008

CHATTERBOX
The New York Dolls — *Too Much Too Soon*
Mercury: 1974

AT THE CLOSE OF A BOOK, AFTER SO MANY WORDS—SOME ERRANT, SOME extraneous, but some, I hope, warranted and wise—I must pay tribute to people who don't seem to need language as a constant companion. A few summers ago, my wife and I sent my kids to stay with my parents for a week. The day we went to pick them up, friends of my parents visited the house with their adult daughter, who was probably twenty-five, maybe a bit older. We had met a few times before. While the rest of us had conversations that ranged from polite and boring to exciting and impolite, she remained quiet. Not off to herself, exactly. She stood near us. She held a beer. But she was very quiet, almost like a tree.

Later on, after the guests left, the rest of us were talking, and someone wondered if the woman had felt uncomfortable with the group. My mother then proceeded to speculate. Had we come on too strong? Had we said something to offend her? Maybe she was having a hard summer.

Maybe she was sick. Maybe that morning a cat had climbed up onto her face and gotten her tongue. "But then we'd see claw marks," my younger son said. (He is not quiet, generally.) We came to no conclusion.

Later, I was sitting in a room with my dad, who wasn't saying anything, and I found it didn't bother me at all. My dad was reading and he set the book down. I thought he was going to talk. He didn't. He went out to the porch to look at some trees. If you ask a quiet person to explain the content of their silence—which seems like at least a minor paradox—they will tell you that there are plenty of other possible explanations. For starters, they might be switched over to receiving instead of broadcasting, communing rather than communicating. That was the case with my father, and it's also the case in John Prine's "Quiet Man" (1972).

> Oodles of light, what a beautiful sight
> Both of God's eyes are shining tonight
> Rays and beams of incredible dreams, and I am a quiet
>   man

I love this song because it is from John Prine's first album, and I love that album, but I also love it because it slows me down before I judge quiet people too harshly. Maybe they're seeing rays and beams of incredible dreams. My father was looking at trees.

In other words, I am suggesting that there are at least two kinds of quiet, and that outward silence is not always indicative of an inner void—or, for that matter, an inner turmoil. There is a third alternative: silence on the outside and balance on the inside. I saw Van Morrison in concert last year, and when he wasn't singing, he was wordless. Silence preoccupies Morrison; he has written about it several times and even titled an album *Hymns to the Silence*. Often it is not the absence of sound so much as the presence of peace, as he attests in "So Quiet in Here" (1990).

> *Oh this must be what it's all about*
> *This must be what paradise is like*
> *So quiet in here, so peaceful in here*

Morrison makes a compelling case for paradise, but is less straightforward on the matter of quiet. For starters, he's not alone; the first four lines seem to suggest so, but then, out of nowhere, there's another heart beating close to his. So shouldn't he be talking to that other heart? In company, you circulate. As it turns out, he is, but with music rather than simple language, since he seems to believe that the words used to describe events and experiences (as opposed to the events and experiences themselves) aren't meaningfully connected to any vital essence: to spirit, to love, to infinities. He doesn't want quiet so much as purer sound. And that purer sound comes from renouncing impurities.

> *All my struggling in the world*
> *And so many dreams that don't come true*
> *Step back, put it all away*
> *It don't matter, it don't matter anymore*

Quiet doesn't have to mean "quiescent." Every classic rock band, every factory that produced gigantic sounds, had a division devoted to quiet. In the Who, John Entwistle was the quiet one, like George Harrison was in the Beatles and Charlie Watts was in the Stones. (Our research department suggests that Charlie Watts may in fact be mute.) But Entwistle was quiet like a pro basketball guard is short, quiet because he wasn't a lead guitarist like Pete Townshend, a lead singer like Roger Daltrey, or an explosive drummer and a compulsive clown like Keith Moon. On "The Quiet One" (1981), he insists on this context and makes a case that he is doing more with less.

I ain't never had time for words that don't rhyme
My head is in a cloud
I ain't quiet, everybody else is too loud

Again, this doesn't go a long way toward vindicating the quiet woman in my parents' house. There's not much evidence that she, like Entwistle, wanted to be understood if not exactly heard. Are there malignant forms of silence? Fred Eaglesmith thinks so. "Quietly" (2008), from the excellent album *Tinderbox*, starts off as a love song. There's no talking and only a little movement. The whole thing happens in slow motion.

Quietly, her hair falls across her pillow
Quietly, she stirs in the morning light
Quietly, she stares up at the ceiling
Then she sits up and she looks into my eyes

Silence can be sexy if it's postcoital, or precoital—or coital, for that matter, where too much blather and funny accents can be distracting. Eaglesmith's song starts sexy like that, but then there's a turn for the worse. The woman's quiet is exposed as neither wonder (as in the Prine song), nor proximity that shames language (as in the Morrison), nor preparation for powerful expression (as in the Entwistle). It's just silence, at least self-absorbed, probably sullen, and even a little punishing. It turns out that she's miserable and planning to leave. Interestingly, the man who is singing the song is so exhausted by her inability to express herself, by the way her silence suggests blame and abandons him, that he lets her go.

Many people have sounded off about silence. Adrienne Rich said, "Lying is done with words but also with silence." It can also be used to tell the truth disreputably, as Fred Eaglesmith suggests. At the same time, there are plenty of people over the course of the planet's history who have lionized silence. Sam Rayburn said, "No one has a finer command of language than the person who keeps his mouth shut." But I don't think I agree with Sam Rayburn, who got to say what he wanted to when he wanted to. I tend to agree with Francis Bacon, who said, "Silence is the virtue of fools."

Once, years ago, I went on a date with a woman, and it went well, and so we went on a second date. On the second date, she said nothing, or nearly nothing. We sat and had a drink. I remember asking her if she was okay, and she said, "Yes," and I think she may even have meant it, but I wasn't okay with the way in which she was okay. I was afraid of what her silence meant, and when I overcame my fear, I found that I was angry at her for presuming that silence was the best that could pass between us. I felt like the silence could have been romantic tension but wasn't. It could have been unconditional agreement, but it wasn't. What it was, in the end, was comfort. That made me afraid and then later angry. I remember thinking that language was imperfect but that silence was the perfect crime.

The woman from the porch remained mysterious to me.

The other friends who spoke to me, in this book, in this life—they passed in and out, through periods of closeness and periods of distance—were not mysterious to me. They were meaningful to me. They were important to me and remain so. I have tried to shine a little light through songs.

The woman from the date: Her, I married.

INDEX BY ARTIST

INDEX BY SONG TITLE

G

H

I

ABOUT THE AUTHOR

Photo © Gail Ghezzi

BEN GREENMAN IS A CONTRIBUTING WRITER TO THE *NEW YORKER* AND the author of eight books of fiction. His most recent novel is *The Slippage*, and his latest collection of short stories is *What He's Poised to Do*. He has collaborated with Questlove on the *New York Times* bestselling hip-hop memoir *Mo' Meta Blues* and on *Something to Food About*, which explores the intersection of creativity and eating, and he also cowrote George Clinton's memoir, *Brothas Be, Yo Like George, Ain't That Funkin' Kinda Hard on You?*, and Brian Wilson's memoir, *I Am Brian Wilson*.